Mrs R.A. J⋯ ⋯ ⋯

General editor: Graham Han⋯

Brodie's Notes on John Fowles's

The French Lieutenant's Woman

Graham Handley MA Ph.D.
Formerly Principal Lecturer in English, College of All Saints, Tottenham

Pan Books London, Sydney and Auckland

For Anne, with love

Acknowledgement My thanks to Jonathan Cape Ltd and the author, John Fowles for permission to reproduce extracts from The French Lieutenant's Woman (© John Fowles 1969)

First published 1988 by Pan Books Ltd
This revised edition published 1990 by Pan Books Ltd,
Cavaye Place, London SW10 9PG
9 8 7 6 5 4 3 2 1
© Pan Books Ltd 1990
ISBN 0 330 50294 8
Photoset by Parker Typesetting Service, Leicester
Printed and bound in Great Britain by
Richard Clay Ltd, Bungay, Suffolk

Contents

Page references are to the Pan edition of *The French Lieutenant's Woman* but as references are also given to particular chapters, the Notes may be used with any edition of the book.

Preface

The intention throughout this study aid is to stimulate and guide, to encourage your involvement in the book, and to develop informed responses and a sure understanding of the main details.

Brodie's Notes provide a clear outline of the play or novel's plot, followed by act, scene, or chapter summaries and/or commentaries. These are designed to emphasize the most important literary and factual details. Poems, stories or non-fiction texts combine brief summary with critical commentary on individual aspects or common features of the genre being examined. Textual notes define what is difficult or obscure and emphasize literary qualities. Revision questions are set at appropriate points to test your ability to appreciate the prescribed book and to write accurately and relevantly about it.

In addition, each of these Notes includes a critical appreciation of the author's art. This covers such major elements as characterization, style, structure, setting and themes. Poems are examined technically – rhyme, rhythm, for instance. In fact, any important aspect of the prescribed work will be evaluated. The aim is to send you back to the text you are studying.

Each study aid concludes with a series of general questions which require a detailed knowledge of the book: some of these questions may invite comparison with other books, some will be suitable for coursework exercises, and some could be adapted to work you are doing on another book or books. Each study aid has been adapted to meet the needs of the current examination requirements. They provide a basic, individual and imaginative response to the work being studied, and it is hoped that they will stimulate you to acquire disciplined reading habits and critical fluency.

Graham Handley 1990

John Fowles and his work

John Fowles was born in 1926. He was educated at Bedford School and Oxford, where he took a degree in French Language and Literature. After a period spent teaching, he became a full-time writer. His first novel was *The Collector* (1963). It is a brilliant and frightening book about a butterfly collector who wins the pools and turns his attention to a young female art student. He collects her, imprisons her, and ultimately ... but no, **you** read it. The novel, which was successfully filmed, established John Fowles as a major force in English fiction. His work has continued to be expressive, innovatory and potently readable. After *The Aristos* (1964) came *The Magus* (1966). This is set on a Greek island and the central character, a schoolmaster, suffers a number of strange and frightening experiences. It is a complex but riveting novel, full of twists and turns. *The French Lieutenant's Woman* (1969) has been called an historical novel but, as you will see, this in no way defines the skill and continuing complexity of Fowles's narrative method. The important and successful screenplay derived from it was by the outstanding modern dramatist Harold Pinter, and this is considered in a separate section of this book (see p.9). *The Ebony Tower* (1974) is a collection of stories which reflect Fowles's remarkable versatility. *Daniel Martin* (1977) is a long and complex book set in a variety of places, but again it is compelling because of its narrative intensity. The rich texture of the book is reflected in the themes which fall within its scope: the brilliant self-analysis by the central character; the psychological intensity; the investigation of relationships – of love and jealousy; the nature of art and of society. Finally there is *Mantissa* (1982), which has been described as an 'extended erotic fantasy' ... 'with mythological undertones'.

On the back cover of *The French Lieutenant's Woman* there are the usual selected snippets of praise, one of which says: 'it is a passionate piece of writing as well as an immaculate example of storytelling.' This sums up Fowles's manner and his art. It is very difficult to think of another modern writer who is as compelling as Fowles – though some would argue for the highly consistent

Iris Murdoch or the Kingsley Amis of *The Old Devils*. We want to know *passionately* what is going to happen to Sarah, for the woman who becomes the New Woman is at the heart of this book. The whole story is tense with expectation, with poignancy, sometimes with humour (black or white), but always with the driving force of narrative. We are aware of Fowles's intellect and the meticulously researched background to the novel, but we are also aware of his radical and sympathetic identification with his characters. The characters come alive, even when they live as revoltingly as Mrs Poulteney. Although the author's voice sounds the genuine note of hindsight, we are conscious of his own involvement with his creations, despite the playing with alternative situations and possibilities. *The French Lieutenant's Woman*, like most of Fowles's work, is major fiction: that is, it is a brilliant blend of the imagination and the intellect which explores and articulates life into art.

The screenplay

In his foreword to the screenplay John Fowles describes its chequered history, referring to the playwright Robert Bolt's feeling that the book was unfilmable, and then telling us that an anonymous writer declined it since it was 'so biased to the female side'. Pinter, a distinguished playwright himself, undertook to write the script. Fowles himself rightly draws attention to the fact that novels are about so much – feelings, emotions, thoughts – which cannot be conveyed as effectively visually as they can verbally. He also emphasises the fact that his novel is written from the mid-Victorian attitude but inlaid with a twentieth-century perspective and, of course, hindsight. If you read the screenplay, or are lucky enough to see the film or video, you will notice (a) the superb economy of the dialogue and (b) the wonderful sense of the locale. You will also see the cuts Pinter has made in the original: note too the *changes* he has made in the interests of condensing the outlines of the story so that they stand out clearly. You will, of course, particularly focus on the major change – that of writing in Mike and Anna in 1979. Another interesting emphasis is on past as well as present time. Is the dramatic impact as great as it is in the book, particularly with regard to 'poor Tragedy'? It will be obvious to you that the screenplay can in no way stand for the book, nor should it. Enjoy it, compare it (insofar as two representations as different as these two can be compared) and then study the book for what it is – a brilliantly sustained representation in its own right.

Introduction – the Victorian novel

The French Lieutenant's Woman is set in the period between March 1867 and the end of May 1869. Fowles's choice of time is very deliberate, as you will see from references in the text to particular events, both cultural and political. We must also consider the novel's time as reflecting the current novel practice, for Fowles uses two techniques which are employed by the novelists of the time. There is no doubt that this is deliberate too, and that in a sense Fowles is writing a Victorian-type novel using the conventions of the period but from a twentieth-century vantage point. The main conventions are the author's use of his own voice and the use of mottoes or epigraphs.

The author's use of his own voice

This runs throughout the Victorian novel. The great writers of the period are Charles Dickens (1812–70), William Makepeace Thackeray (1811–63), Elizabeth Gaskell (1810–65), George Eliot (1819–80), Anthony Trollope (1815–83) and Thomas Hardy (1840–1928). Hardy is much present in the narrative of Fowles's novel, primarily as a poet. In this sense he will be examined later in this introduction. All these authors use their own voices, some more than others, so much so that they often succeed in becoming a character in their own novels. I am not talking about first-person narrative – the technique which is used with telling immediacy in, for example, *David Copperfield* and *Great Expectations* and in two of Charlotte Brontë's novels, *Jane Eyre* and *Villette*. I have omitted Charlotte Brontë (1816–55) from the list above although she is certainly a great writer, because it doesn't seem to me that, with the exception of the status of women, she has any connection with Fowles at all. Her sister Emily (1818–48) has even less, since her great novel *Wuthering Heights* is beyond Victorian time and place in its conception. Dickens's use of his voice varies greatly, but for the most part it is heard in social and moral condemnation of the evils of society. A good example occurs in *Bleak House*, where Dickens inveighs against church, state and the privileged in general on the death of Jo the crossing-sweeper. That death exemplifies the extreme of poverty in Victorian society, something which Fowles touches on from time to time in his narrative.

Thackeray in *Vanity Fair* uses his voice in ironic comment on character and situation, sometimes drawing the puppet analogy with his created characters. This is a tone often adopted by Fowles, who goes farther and teases the reader about the control of his characters, so much so that he even writes about courses they have taken when in fact they haven't – clear demonstration of his control and manipulation. Barbara Hardy, one of the best critics of our own time, has written tellingly about the skill with which George Eliot indicates the alternative lives her characters might have led. George Eliot, who lived unmarried with George Henry Lewes for twenty-four years until his death, often makes moral comments in her writing and urges the course of duty, something which Fowles picks up in his own text by referring to one of her celebrated statements on that theme. Mrs Gaskell, wife of a Unitarian minister, employs her voice in the interest of Christian reconciliation of conflict, while Trollope uses his, rather like Thackeray, in ironic contemplation of character and situation. Hardy, through to the end of his career, uses his own voice in judgement of the evils which are practised in the name of society and religion. Thus when Tess Durbeyfield is hanged for the murder of her lover Alec D'Urberville, Hardy leaves us in no doubt about his views. It is one of the most celebrated assertions of the period (in fact as late as 1891): '"Justice" was done, and the President of the Immortals (in Aeschylean phrase) had finished his sport with Tess.' The author's voice is trenchant with a cynical fatalism.

John Fowles uses this convention – sometimes referred to as the omniscient author convention – fully, orchestrating his text with a range of individual notes. Like the writers of the period, he uses a number of learned references. Like them, he comments on important events of the day – the influence of Darwin, the Second Reform Bill of 1867, or J. S. Mill's attempts to raise the status of women. Fowles makes it quite clear that he is a radical, and that Sarah, handicapped and abused because she is a woman, is symbolic of individuality and women's rights. I have mentioned one of his favourite devices, and this is to tease the reader by suggesting what his characters did do, and then having them do the reverse. Once you have got used to the convention, you might note one important effect – it serves to remind us that we are reading fiction, which holds up the mirror to reality but can never be reality itself.

The mottoes or epigraphs

You will notice that Fowles uses a motto or epigraph – or two – before each chapter. They make a comment, either in their subject matter or through general association, on the events of the chapter concerned, for example, on the situation or character. The idea of using mottoes which are effectively an extension of the text begins with Sir Walter Scott (1771–1832) in *Waverley* (1814). His use is not a sophisticated one – the quotations, snatches of song or ballad, are largely ornamental rather than part of the structure of the novel. Dickens, Trollope, Thackeray all ignore the usage, while Hardy very occasionally employs it in his earlier work. But Mrs Gaskell and George Eliot both employ the motto to good effect. I demonstrated in an article written some years ago that the mottoes used by Mrs Gaskell in her novel *Mary Barton* (1848) are an integral part of her text, a deliberate running commentary on the poverty, deprivation and suffering of her characters in the Hungry Forties about which she is writing. And by the time we get to George Eliot, the usage is refined so much that the mottoes are required reading if you want to understand the full range of reference she is undertaking in her dedicated and intellectual narrative modes. By a curious time coincidence, she first begins to use mottoes in *Felix Holt* (1865–6), published just before the fictional time of John Fowles's novel. Sometimes, she even writes the mottoes herself: when she doesn't, her range of association through quotation is an impressive one – from the Bible, Shakespeare, the classical authors and foreign writers as well.

There is little doubt that John Fowles's usage of mottoes is not merely lip-service to a Victorian convention. The choice of writers and works and the associations they set up is deliberate and fascinating. There is not space either here or in the textual notes to comment on all of them, but a selection of the most important is commented on below in some detail. As you read, look at each of the mottoes used and see if you can relate them either to the chapter you are about to read or to the more general concerns and situations of the novel. Those which are factual reports of the Victorian period or aspects of it generally carry their own obvious message or comment.

Hardy Mottoes from Hardy, the great radical writer of the late Victorian period, are almost a natural corollary to the text. Hardy was virtually to abandon fiction in 1895 after the critical abuse of *Jude the Obscure* (called by one critic 'Jude the Obscene') and returned to his first love, poetry. The mottoes here are from the poems, and they vary in tone from the lightness of love, a certain nostalgia for past time, sense of loss, poignant memory. This is by no means to indicate Hardy's range, but merely to show how these fit into the pattern and situations of *The French Lieutenant's Woman*. Hardy's wife died in 1912 and, although he remarried, he poured out a number of poems expressive of loss and love for the wife who, in their lifetime, he had not appreciated. The poems recapture time past with poignant effect.

Tennyson Tennyson became Poet Laureate in 1850, and in Fowles's novel *In Memoriam* and *Maud* are referred to often. The first poem – one of the great poems of the age – is Tennyson's long elegiac expression of his love for his best friend, Arthur Henry Hallam, who had died in Vienna in 1833 aged 22. The poem was sixteen years in the making, and although the stanza form is regular, the different moods, thoughts, beliefs, recognitions and the overall terrible sense of loss reflect both the individual suffering and some of the main concerns of the period as well. Tennyson sets down his thoughts on evolution and the question of immortality, his doubts perhaps more strongly expressed than his faith. It was a great popular success, running into many editions. I am not suggesting that there is a direct link with Charles, though he certainly has his doubts, but I do feel that the poem reflects the crisis of Victorian faith, and that the novel we are reading reflects too the twists and turns of belief and scepticism in the period. *Maud* is much different in kind. It was written in 1854 and published in 1855 (it is thus contemporary with the Crimean War). It is a morbid story, and it aroused some critical controversy at the time because of its theme that shedding blood is a cure for disappointed love. It is of interest here (the narrator, like Charles, goes abroad but becomes mad) because of its obvious fascination for John Fowles. There is a strong streak of morbidity in Sarah – arguably her disappointment in love has made her mad, and there is madness too in the family – and this is a direct imaginative connection. *Maud* is, I think, underrated despite its thematic unpleasantness: and some of the lyrics, the finest Tennyson ever wrote, reflect an ecstasy which Charles and Sarah, albeit temporarily, share.

A. H. Clough (1819–61) Again one of Fowles's favourite points of reference in the mottoes. He too was filled with doubt and uncertainty in the wake of the Oxford Movement (see textual note). His poetry is often experimental in form, expressive of love, doubt, duty and sometimes of a kind of paralysis which denies commitment. Clough thought of himself as a failure: the mottoes in some ways reflect the doubts and uncertainties of Charles.

Matthew Arnold (1822–88) Educated like Clough at Rugby (his father Thomas was the Headmaster) and Balliol College Oxford, Arnold is one of the great Victorian influences. Poet, school inspector, important prose writer of criticism, social and educational concerns, Arnold married in 1851 and had six children. The mottoes in this novel are taken from the Marguerite sequence of his poems and reflect an unknown love (though there have been plenty of attempts at identification). 'Yes! in the sea of life enisled . . .' is quoted not as motto but in the text (a note is given on it). Once again, we can see the connection with the situation of Charles and Sarah.

Jane Austen – Persuasion If the setting of *The French Lieutenant's Woman* evokes Hardy (Lyme Regis is well inside Hardy's Wessex), then it also carries immediate associations with Jane Austen's *Persuasion*, which was published in 1818 after her death the previous year. It is at Lyme Regis that Louisa, jumping down the Cobb to be caught by Captain Wentworth, falls and injures herself. Wentworth takes upon himself the blame for the accident. The irony of this is, that although Wentworth was initially attracted to Louisa, he had found himself greatly appreciating Anne Elliot, with whom he had been in love some years previously. She has always cared for him, but had been forced to reject him by family pressure. A 'fallen woman' on the Cobb therefore carries obvious ironic overtones, and there is some echo on a social level in the polite conversation between Charles,

Ernestina and Mrs Tranter. Fowles himself has something of Jane Austen's ironic appraisal of life, but it would be wrong, I think, to read too much into the *Persuasion* associations. The location makes any analogy at once limited and natural.

Other mottoes As I have said earlier, these are scattered and have their own particular importance. Darwin's importance within the period after 1859 cannot be exaggerated. Fowles does not merely use him in mottoes, but in the text itself, as you will remember from the debate between Grogan and Charles. The constant reiteration of the dates of the time is important, and the mottoes, with their content taken from the 1840s or 1850s, often reflect the doubts before Darwin, doubts which he himself was to crystallize through his conclusions.

Note Victorian novels from *Pickwick Papers* (1836) onwards were often issued in serial form before being published in one or more volumes. John Fowles is manifestly writing a continuous narrative, and is not concerned with Victorian modes of publication. Both his tone and his formal practice capture the spirit, but built into it is a kind of irony. This is not condescending but, given the radical concerns of the writing, inevitable.

Chapter commentaries, textual notes, revision questions

Chapter 1

We note immediately the scene setting, the central location (much beloved by the author), some unusual vocabulary (a feature of Fowles's style), and the exactness of the date. There is a certain historical sense, some figurative language ('that largest bite ... south-western leg'). Fowles is writing a Victorian novel with twentieth-century psychological insight. He does what Victorian writers so often did – he uses his own voice just as the Victorian giants Dickens, Thackeray and George Eliot, for example, did. We register too Fowles's visual imagination, successfully translated in the screenplay, from the broad landscape perspective down to the exact clothes of the young lady and gentleman and the black impression of the third figure. The writing is vivid, arresting, with a fine sense of expectation aroused by the close of the chapter.

motto: Hardy Note how perfectly this quotation captures the perspective of 'poor Tragedy' who soon becomes known to us as Sarah Woodruff.

the late march of 1867 Note this date, and try to work out the exact chronology of the novel as you read. The year is significant for the passing of the Second Reform Bill.

The Cobb Significant location. Louisa Musgrove falls here in Jane Austen's *Persuasion* (1818) in Chapter XII.

Piraeus The main port of Athens.

the Armada The Spanish fleet sent by Philip II to attack England in 1588. It was defeated in the Channel.

Monmouth (1649–85) The illegitimate son of Charles II. He rashly tried to seize the throne after his father's death by landing with rebel forces in Dorset. He was defeated at Sedgemoor, captured and executed in 1685.

Henry Moore Celebrated twentieth-century sculptor (1898–1987).

Michelangelo (1475–1564) The great Italian Renaissance painter, poet and sculptor, celebrated in particular for his frescoes in the Sistine Chapel, Rome.

I exaggerate? Get accustomed to the author's use of his own voice. It is one of his main techniques (see Introduction, page 10).

another wind was blowing in 1867 Fowles is playing on Harold

Macmillan's famous 'wind of change' remark to underline ironically the change in fashion in the 1860s.

revetment (Usually in a fortification), wall.

dundrearies Long side whiskers but no beard, the term taken from Lord Dundreary, a character in a comedy by Tom Taylor (1858) – Fowles is carefully authenticating the period by such a reference.

A figure from myth Note the emphasis here, which at once establishes Sarah as extraordinary (Charles is later to say 'remarkable') before we meet her.

Chapter 2

Again note the importance, the direct significance of the two mottoes, the first focusing on superfluous women (part of a theme in this novel), the second acting as anticipation of the situation of Sarah Woodruff. The chapter moves into dialogue, giving us the dramatic and essentially romantic interaction between Charles and Tina. There is banter, punning, and topical discussion with Tina's father's bias over that epoch-shattering *On the Origin of Species*. Charles even indulges some irony at his own expense. Obviously fossils are his passion. There is an authorial aside about the class differences in Victorian society. Narrative excitement quickens when Tina – occasionally elevated to Ernestina – and Charles contemplate the black figure. The ensuing dialogue tells in bare outline the story of 'poor Tragedy ... the French Lieutenant's Woman'. When Charles tries to help the girl, her look through him shows just how self-absorbed she is. This capacity for self-absorption, for isolation, is one of Sarah's distinguishing habits. Note particularly the vivid single-word description of Sarah and the poetic quality of the language too – we are meeting a strongly individualized and unusual Victorian heroine. The emphasis on the 'madness' being elsewhere shows how individualistic the presentation is. It is heightened because of Sarah's silence.

motto: West-Country Folksong – my false love will weep... Notice how this resonates in the text – Sarah weeps, Charles later weeps (and is false in a sense), Ernestina weeps ... and in a curious way, because of her lies, Sarah *is* false (the French Lieutenant is too).

dry a stick ... stick-y ... glued Clever-clever superficial punning, a telling contrast with some of the intense language to come.

over the port i.e. the convention was for the men to stay and drink port after the meal while the women withdrew – an indication of the subordinate position of women which is examined in the novel. But remember Mrs Poulteney!

Mr Darwin Charles Darwin (1809–82) *On the Origin of Species by Means of Natural Selection* (1859). The earth-shattering book which argued for the natural rather than the divine origin of species, advancing a theory of evolution which accepted change and allowed for the development of new species, the survival of the fittest. Darwin was to arouse even greater religious opposition by his later *The Descent of Man* (1871), which traced man's origin to the ancestors of gorillas and chimpanzees.

'*Et voilà tout*' And that's all.

'I have written a monograph, so I must be.' Charles is being ironic about his achievements and status.

oolite Distinctive rock.

Jane Austen made Louisa Musgrove . . . See note to Chapter One, page 16.

. . . Woman The dots perhaps indicate that Tina has heard the word 'whore' but doesn't like to let Charles know that she has.

That was out of oblivion i.e. she was oblivious to, ignorant of, current fashion.

the favoured feminine look . . . Note the ironic tone.

that look as a lance i.e. it pierced him, as it is to do often later.

Chapter 3

Charles is brooding about life and about the unwelcome prospect of a wet afternoon. The author directs us to consider the different attitudes towards time then (1867) and now, with people in our own time oppressively aware of its pressures. A superb space image of 'colonnades' (page 16) makes us aware of the way time appeared to be spread – and needed to be filled – in the Victorian period. John Fowles brings historical perspective to bear on this period. There is the quietly effective focus on Karl Marx working towards the major change of the twentieth century – communism. Charles's own leisured background is investigated, while the incident of his shooting the Great Bustard is a comic one. Charles's moral and spiritual movements are described, but his own irony and intelligence combine to make him 'a healthy agnostic' (page 18). His habits, regarded by the conventional as eccentric, are described, together with his interest in palaeontology and his non-political stance. He is inherently lazy and aware of his own lack of stature in this richest period of Victorian cultural and scientific interest. But he has travelled much and been courted much by Victorian mammas in the interests of their daughters. Charles is outwardly cynical.

motto: Darwin This reflects directly on Sarah, who is almost born out of her time in terms of her acute individuality.

adagio Leisurely.

the vast colonnades of leisure Space image used to define an extended measure of time.

1848 The year of revolution in the major capitals of Europe.

Chartists Largely working-class movement (1837–48) whose demands were presented in the *People's Charter* (1838) which sought among other things votes for all adult males, voting by ballot, annual parliament and salaries for MPs.

the beavered German Jew Karl Marx (1818–83) wrote *Das Kapital* in 1867. He was effectively the founder of Communism.

red fruit i.e. in Bolshevik Russia with the Revolution of 1917 and Lenin coming to power. The Tsars were finally overthrown.

Almack's Founded by William Almack (died 1781). They were assembly rooms in St James's, London, which housed a gambling club.

in tail male Settlement of succession of landed estate to male heir(s) only.

the Thirty-nine Articles These were first drawn up in 1562. All candidates for ordination in the Church of England have to subscribe to them, as does any clergyman taking a new benefice.

Oxford Movement–Roman Catholicism *propria terra* The Latin phrase means 'own country'. The Oxford Movement was the Anglican High Church Movement which set out to restore the ideals and ritual of the seventeenth-century church. It began in 1833 with a series of 'Tracts for the Times'. Its important founders were Keble and John Henry Newman, the latter defecting to Catholicism later, as did some of his followers, hence the remark here.

City of Sin London.

infra dig. Unbecoming, beneath one's dignity.

conversazioni Social evening given by a learned society.

Gladstone (1809–98) The great Liberal leader who was Prime Minister on four occasions, the last time 1892–4.

with Macaulay so close behind Thomas Babington Macaulay (1800–59) the great historian and essayist who exerted a profound influence on the Victorian period.

the greatest galaxy of talent in the history of English literature For example, Dickens, the Brontës, Thackeray, George Eliot, Trollope, Tennyson, Browning etc. Hardy does not begin to publish fiction successfully until 1872.

Lyell Sir Charles Lyell (1797–1875) the great geologist who revolutionized ideas about the age of the earth and established the idea of a gradual process of natural law.

Disraeli Benjamin, first Earl of Beaconsfield (1804–81), major statesman of the period, twice Prime Minister and a successful novelist.

Byronic ennui ... Byronic outlets: genius and adultery Note the

epigrammatic turn of the last phrase. Byron (1788–1824), the English
romantic poet who greatly influenced European thought. Always
involved in scandal but capable of great idealism.

the hidden teeth of the matrimonial traps The image is taken up
factually by the reference to Mrs Poulteney's precautions to stop any
young man from passing through the gardens of Marlborough House.

Chapter 4

The description of Mrs Poulteney's Regency house is overlaid
with satire about the perpetual fires and the decor. Though Mrs
Fairley is described, the emphasis in the chapter is on the tyranny of Mrs Poulteney, and the intolerable working hours and
conditions of her servants. The phrase which best defines the
two women is that they are 'incipient sadists' (page 22). The
man-traps indicate Mrs Poulteney's obsession in the name of
Christianity, and her charity – what a mockery of the word she
is! – is much respected. Fowles here uses retrospect to fill in the
details of her taking in the French Lieutenant's Woman. The
focus on the vicar shows his hypocrisy and the Low Church
practice of the period, which is accurately documented by the
reference to the cholera outbreak of 1865. There is much irony
at the expense of Mrs Poulteney, her idea of storing up favour
for herself in heaven resting on how much she 'gives' down here
on earth. Through the manipulation of the vicar, who is also
viewed ironically, she takes on, or rather over, Sarah Woodruff.
But before he gets his way over this the vicar has pushed Mrs
Poulteney in the direction he knows will be efficacious – he has
fanned her flames of jealousy with regard to Lady Cotton.

motto: Mrs Norton Mrs Norton is referred to in some detail in Chapter
16 (pages 99–110).

motto: Royston Pike – lived above their own cesspool i.e. as
Londoners did, above the polluted, contaminated Thames.

this Stygian domain i.e. murky, gloomy, black, after the river Styx
(Hades) in classical mythology.

But when you are expected to rise at six ... Note how much social
(and moral) comment Fowles gets into this novel – here the appalling
conditions of a great number of the working class of the period are
described.

like some plump vulture ... Note the immediate, unchristian and
predatory nature of this blunt image.

humane man-traps See note above.

the Gestapo The German – Nazi – secret police who wielded enormous power during Hitler's rule from 1933–45.

the ascendant British Empire Again a period notation, for the mid-to-late nineteenth century witnesses the expansion of British interests in, for example, India and Africa.

which side his pastoral bread was buttered Fowles is the master of the commonplace image, but invests it with a particular ironic tone.

Romish cancer i.e. the influence of Roman Catholicism (see note page 19).

enounced i.e. enunciated, pronounced (rarely used now).

fourth great cholera onslaught Another piece of documentation and another underlining of the incidence of disease in nineteenth-century England.

the face of the Duke of Wellington Arthur Wellesley, 1st Duke (1769–1852), the victor of Waterloo (1815), Prime Minister (1828–30), influential English statesman.

de haut en bas From high to low.

like a black opal Note the vivid effect of this image.

eleemosynary i.e. dependent on alms, charity.

Chapter 5

An ironic account of the Victorian femininity of Ernestina, but with hints of some difference. Literary and illustrative references contribute to the tone of the description. This is followed by another kind of ironic description, that is of the objects in Aunt Tranter's house. The irony continues with an account of the oppressively spoilt nature of Ernestina's life – the poor little rich girl trap. The author's voice reminds us of the advantages of hindsight and the control of his characters' destiny in his comment on Ernestina's long life. The tone is witty, as when Ernestina is called 'an English Juliet with her flat-footed nurse' (page 29). There is an insight into Ernestina's awakening sexuality (and the fears this brings with it in the period in which she lives), some egoistic self-contemplation, and another period emphasis when she takes out the girl's best friend – her diary.

motto: Tennyson See section on *The Victorian Novel* – page 10 of this commentary.

motto: Jane Austen From *Persuasion* Chapter 11.

Phiz's work or John Leech's The first the pseudonym of Hablot K. Browne (1815–82), celebrated illustrator of Dickens: the second another famous Victorian illustrator who worked for *Punch* (1817–64).

Becky Sharp The brilliant, captivating, unscrupulous adventuress of
Thackeray's *Vanity Fair* (1848).
Prinny, George IV (1762–1830) Reigned 1820–30, earlier notorious
for his good living and amorous affairs.
bouderies Sulks.
consumptive i.e. suffering from tuberculosis.
the day that Hitler invaded Poland 1 September 1939.
Juliet ... Romeo the young lovers, ill-starred, in Shakespeare's *Romeo
and Juliet* (1595).
a *peignoir* Loose dressing-gown.
Laocoön embrace Laocoön was the Trojan priest who warned of the
wooden horse by which the Greeks entered Troy: he was crushed to
death by two serpents.

Chapter 6

The resumption of the conversation between the vicar and the
revolting Mrs Poulteney. The function of the vicar in this chapter is to give Mrs Poulteney – and thus the reader – a full
account of Sarah. The retrospect provides the story, and reveals
the psychological influences which have shaped Sarah's present
behaviour. The narrowness of outlook is seen in Mrs Poulteney's
horror that Sarah speaks French: that talent apparently carried
in the Victorian age overtones of corruption. The vicar knows
exactly how to butter up Mrs Poulteney in order to get her to
take in Sarah. The character of the French Lieutenant is spelled
out. The vicar takes upon himself the definition of Sarah's state,
that is, she is suffering from a fixed delusion (i.e. that the
Lieutenant is honourable and will return). Note the emphasis on
Mrs Poulteney's motivation – she wants to be one up on Lady
Cotton. We also register that the really Christian behaviour
comes from Mrs Talbot, who does not condemn Sarah's
behaviour. In turn the reader is invited to view the qualities in
Sarah's behaviour which appeal to Mrs Poulteney, who interprets them in the way she wants to. There is grim humour in
Mrs Poulteney's choice of a Biblical passage for Sarah to read.
The chapter ends superbly with a brief indication of Sarah's
dual motives in wishing to be in Mrs Poulteney's house.

motto: Maud One of Fowles's favourite poems (see the section in this
commentary on *The Victorian Novel*).
the Good Samaritan Luke x: 29–37.

'She speaks French?' This acquirement, outside polite ladies' conversation, was thought to indicate loose living.

Patmos The Greek island where, according to legend, St John lived in exile and saw the visions of the apocalypse.

Dies Irae Day of Anger.

the egregious McLuhan The American scholar who coined the famous phrase 'The medium is the message'.

Chapter 7

A fine opening paragraph describes the nature of the day, the optimism and feeling of well-being which it kindles in Charles. The interaction between Sam and Charles is humorous, and Sam's aggressiveness over the girl covers the direction his heart will take towards her. Charles enjoys punning at Sam's expense. His contemplation of himself in the mirror before shaving is equivalent to Ernestina's self-examination earlier. The account of Sam's character which follows is intent on making Sam a 'character'. The literary analogy with Sam Weller is drawn, this Sam being a sharp, fast, cockney dandy. The authorial voice indulges itself on the question of cockney pronunciation, and then goes on to explain the natural bond between Sam and Charles. Charles is quite simply amused by him. Whether we are amused by the self-conscious authorial voice is another matter.

a kind of Proustian richness of evocation The reference is to The great novel *Remembrance of Things Past* by Marcel Proust (1871–1922), remarkable for its evocation of time past and for its psychological analysis.

Quod est demonstrandum ... Ergo Which was to be proved ... therefore.

Dahn Down.

Cupid is being unfair to Cockneys Cupid is the Roman God of Love, son of Venus. Note how naturally the phrase is coined here.

gin-palace These abounded in London, and were responsible for much of the drunkenness and debauchery among the working classes.

Hall the Hosslers 'eard All the ostlers heard – Sam is a true cockney in his ability to lose and gain aitches.

Doric The oldest, simplest of the orders of Greek architecture.

sharp Cunning, clever.

the immortal Weller ... *Pickwick Papers* The latter was published in twenty monthly parts April 1836–November 1837, and established Dickens as a major writer. Sam Weller is Mr Pickwick's cheerful, engaging servant, one of the greatest of Dickens's comic creations.

a stage version of it There were no effective laws of copyright at the time, and Dickens's popularity was such that whatever he wrote was plagiarized and staged quickly in order to make money.

Beau Brummel (1778–1840) The favourite of the Prince Regent who was a dandified setter of fashion in the period.

Sancho Panza Don Quixote's common-sense squire and servant in Cervantes' *Don Quixote* (1605 and 1615).

Dorothea The saint who suffered martyrdom in AD 311.

'rose his hibrows' Raised his eyebrows.

Chapter 8

Immediate contrast between Charles and Ernestina, for the latter has had a disturbed night and is not able to greet the day well. Charles is thereby able to follow his palaeontological interests in the leisure suddenly afforded him. There follows considerable authorial commentary on and evaluation of local palaeontology. The description of Charles's dress and equipment contains some irony, but this is tempered by the reflection that although the Victorians were over-dressed and over-equipped they 'laid the foundations of all our modern science' (page 46). The effect of the activity and the landscape on Charles is given a considered stress. Charles is almost tempted – but not quite – to give up London for this kind of life. There is some discussion of the ladder of nature theory and the way in which Darwin has upset it: the corollary to this is Charles's own feeling that he is a Darwinist when of course he isn't completely.

motto: Sketches from Cambridge Leslie Stephen (1832–1904) was the father of Virginia Woolf, one of the great twentieth-century novelists. The quotation applies particularly to himself, for from 1882 onwards he was the editor of *The Dictionary of National Biography*.

Mary Anning (1799–1847) Discovered the Ichthyosaurus skeleton in a cliff near Lyme (1817).

Ichthyosaurus platyodon One of a species of prehistoric monster.

anningii i.e. Her name as part of the scientific name of a species.

striations Ridges, furrows, linear marks on surface.

Baedeker The German publisher (1801–59) who issued a comprehensive series of guidebooks.

duty Fowles has got the sense of what George Eliot (1819–1880) said, but the quotation should read – 'taking as her text . . . the words, *God, Immortality, Duty,* – pronounced with terrible earnestness how inconceivable was the *first*, how unbelievable the *second*, and yet how peremptory and absolute the *third*.'

The Voyage of the Beagle Published, with a rather longer title, in 1839.

oubliette Secret dungeon entered only by a trapdoor above.

Linnaean The Latin form of Carl von Linné (1707–78), Swedish naturalist. His main concerns are evident from the text.

the Swedish fetters i.e. the influence of Linnaeus.

edificiality In the nature of a large or stately building.

exempli gratia Witness the example of.

hopscotched Note the verbal usage, unusual, and showing the vital way in which Fowles uses words.

half-hunter Watch with hinged metal cover (to protect the glass) having a circular opening in it.

Chapter 9

The beginning of the chapter introduces us to Mrs Talbot and gives us insight into her imagination which is influenced by her reading of romantic fiction. Mrs Talbot fears for Sarah's sanity, and is particularly afraid that Sarah might commit suicide. However, her advice is that Sarah should accept the post with Mrs Poulteney. This is followed by a switch to Sarah and her ability to measure the worth of other people – 'she saw them as they were and not as they tried to seem' (page 50). She has a profound insight into human nature, and often judges by the standards of the few great writers she has read. Her father's obsession with ancestry and his subsequent decline into madness are described. Sarah's first brush with Mrs Poulteney occurs, and after this it seems that Sarah knows how to control that tyrannical lady – up to a point. Sarah's voice and the influence it exerts are particularly dwelt on. She even moves Mrs Poulteney to tears on occasions, and is moved herself by her religious reading. Sarah delivers tracts, and the force of her personality is evident. When Sarah's health suffers Mrs Poulteney begrudgingly allows her time off. Sarah shows her tact and diplomacy by her ability to choose whether or not to stay in the room when Mrs Poulteney has company. The tension between Mrs Fairley and Sarah is almost entirely due to Mrs Fairley's jealousy, and the cunning Mrs Fairley becomes a self-appointed spy on Sarah's privacy. As a result, Mrs Poulteney receives information which causes her to reprimand Sarah. Sarah appears to give way to her demands, but the chapter ends on a note of expectation and crisis, with the news that Sarah has taken to walking on Ware Commons.

milieux Environments, surroundings.

Mrs Sherwood's edifying tales Mrs Mary Sherwood (1775–1851)
prolific writer of stories and books of a pious nature for young people.

Paul and Virginia The names would seem to be deliberately chosen –
Paul et Virginie by Bernardin de St Pierre was published in 1788. The
romantic and idealised story of two young children was very popular.

she was born with a computer in her heart Note the modern image to
underline the essential intuitive rightness of Sarah's reactions and
judgements.

Walter Scott and Jane Austen Walter Scott was the great Scots writer
(1771–1832) whose career as a novelist began with *Waverely* (1814).
Jane Austen has already been mentioned – see note page 16.

Drake family i.e. Sir Francis Drake (1540?–96) who sailed round the
world, and helped to defeat the Spanish Armada in 1588.

**The ferns looked greenly forgiving; but Mrs Poulteney was whitely
the contrary** Note the fine epigrammatic quality of this – Fowles often
writes with exquisite balance.

peccadilloes Small, trifling offences.

twigged Seen into and through.

a skilled cardinal, a weak pope Note the irony of the phrase in view of
Mrs Poulteney's Anglicanism.

an unconscious alienation effect of the Brechtian kind Berthold
Brecht (1898–1956) the German dramatist whose theories have
exerted a major influence on twentieth-century drama.

Lama, lama, sabachthane me 'God, my God, why has thou forsaken
me?'

the tract test i.e. willingly distributing religious tracts among the poor.

vis-à-vis In comparison with.

barouche Carriage.

Satan's sails i.e. temptation (in the form of the French Lieutenant's
return).

as the Queen on her throne A deliberate reminder of the period and
the permanent effect of the image of the Queen – Victoria – on the
public consciousness.

Chapter 10

A lyrical and factual account of the coastal landscape, the
Undercliff and its isolation, opens this chapter. The eastern half
is called Ware Commons, and when Charles enters the Undercliff this prepares us for the encounter between Charles and
Sarah. Note the exact date is given. But before that there is
much praise of the Renaissance in art, the scene on the Undercliff being Renaissance in texture and tone. Charles naturally
pursues his scientific interests here for a little while, but he is

arrested by the sight of the figure sleeping, as is the reader. Note that the art analogy is being developed in this 'picture'. Charles is moved by the sight of Sarah, feeling protective, despite the unconscious sexuality of the pose. When she awakes both are aware of the mystical significance of the moment despite their 'mutual incomprehension' (page 65).

mottoes: Tennyson and Jane Austen See section on *The Victorian Novel* page 10.

March 29th 1867 Note again the precise chronology.

Botticelli (1447–1510) Italian Renaissance painter.

Ronsard Pierre de (1524–85), French lyric poet.

Rousseau Jean Jacques (1712–78), the famous French philosopher who believed that man should return to his natural state.

the Golden Age In Greek and Roman mythology, the first and best age of the world, in which man was happy.

And there, below him, he saw a figure. Note how brilliantly effective this sudden sentence is, focusing our attention and Charles's too.

the curving lip of the plateau Note the effective personification and the sensual nature of the image, almost anticipatory of Sarah herself.

locked in a mutual incomprehension Again there is a physicality about the phrase, for despite what it says it suggests their later coming together.

the whole Victorian Age was lost i.e. it is the beginning of Charles's rejection of the conventions which the Victorian Age lived by.

Questions on Chapters 1–10

1 What does the author achieve by using his own voice? You should refer closely to the text in your answer.

2 Basing your answer on what you have read so far, compare and contrast Ernestina and Sarah.

3 What are the main aspects of the author's style in these chapters?

4 What have you learned about the Victorian period from these chapters? (You might refer to Darwin, for example.)

5 Do you find Charles a likeable character or not? Give reasons for your answer.

6 Examine the part played by either Sam *or* Mrs Poulteney in the action so far.

Chapter 11

The time connection with Ernestina is made immediately, thus helping to unify the structure of the novel. Ernestina reveals one of her fears about Charles, which is that he is liable to flirt, but her thoughts show how limited her imagination is and how little she knows him. She has too a natural jealousy of Mary, who is very pretty. Mary has also previously been in the employ of Mrs Poulteney until the latter was offended by her attractiveness. But she certainly gets on well with Mrs Tranter. Mary in her turn envies her mistress, who has all the clothes that she would like. Mary also feels that Charles is too good for Ernestina. Mary is very fond of Sam, and Ernestina as mistress warns her against him because of his 'Don Juan' reputation. There is a neat upstairs/downstairs interaction going on here. This is broken off by a filling in of the social backgrounds, retrospect on Ernestina's suitors and her courtship with Charles who feels that life is passing him by, and decides to settle down with Ernestina. Their coming together is told with rare irony.

motto: A. H. Clough See section on *The Victorian Novel* (page 14).
motto: William Barnes William Barnes (1801–86), the Dorset dialect poet, a friend of Hardy's, who paid generous tribute to him and wrote a poem on his death, 'The Last Signal'.
At approximately the same time . . . Fowles uses links like this as an ironic comment and also to give the novel a unified structure.
grisette French working girl (derived from their being dressed in grey).
Cintra In Portugal.
Occam's useful razor Derived from the philosopher William Occam (c.1300–1349). It refers to the principle that asssumptions which offer an explanation of something cannot be unnecessarily multiplied.
Waterloo a month after Waterloo saw the final defeat of the French under Napoleon by the English under Wellington and the Prussians under Blücher. (18 June 1815).
Flora The Roman goddess of flowers and spring.
Ronsard See note page 27.
rondelet See the author's definition which follows.
who is twenty-two years old . . . Sometimes the authorial tone is cloyingly personal, as if the fictional characters beget characters who live on, though this is perhaps a private joke between author and reader.
soubrettes Here, coquettish maidservants.
à la mode In fashion.
heven Even.

tick i.e. without being paid for until later.

Don Juan The reference is to the legendary lover, a Spanish nobleman who led a dissolute life. The term has become synonymous for a man who has many women.

Lord Brabazon Vavasour Vere de Vere The titles and the actual words sound to be the height of aristocratic descent – but Tina is mocking.

as any modern security department vets its atomic scientists. Again the author's voice is used to indicate the changes between this century and the last.

soirées Evening parties.

the women . . . haunted the doorways round the Haymarket i.e. the prostitutes. This anticipates casually Charles's later significant encounter with the less fashionable prostitute Sarah.

For the rest of my life I shall travel. Ironically, this is what Charles does for some time after he has lost Sarah and rejected Ernestina completely, and not jokingly, as here.

How can you mercilessly imprison all natural sexual instinct . . . This theme of repression is explored throughout the novel.

Chapter 12

Meanwhile we return (the right word) to time present, with Charles in the woods of Ware Commons. His stop at the dairy moves the plot on, since the dairyman knows Sarah, the 'French Loot'n'nts Hoer' (page 77). Narrative excitement builds up as Charles follows the girl. But his attempts at politeness and solicitude are met with a rebuff; Sarah wants to walk alone. He decides to call to see Ernestina by way of reaction. We are invited to contemplate the social niceties and superficialities of Charles and Ernestina in interaction as distinct from the positive and unusual individuality of Sarah. Charles nearly reveals to Ernestina what he has been doing, but has the natural apprehension of knowing that it will displease her. There follows another retrospect – this time on the reputation and the reason for it – of Ware Commons. Confronted by Mrs Poulteney with her 'sin', Sarah cannot understand what she has done wrong, and actually gets away with sarcasm. The irony embraces the fact that Mrs Poulteney has never seen Ware Commons. There is a heavy authorial comment at the close of the chapter, with Sarah weeping alone.

mottoes: Marx and Tennyson Both are relevant to the concerns of the novel, the Tennyson poignantly questioning.

hoying . . . byre i.e. driving beasts to the cowshed.

like squadrons of reserve moons Note the vividness of this, typical of Fowles's lively style.

a Jeremiah Jeremiah was a major Hebrew prophet who foresaw disaster; hence someone who is miserable and who denounces his times.

a dooming stare Economical way of reinforcing the above.

Hoer Whore.

as if she was a figure in a dream This exactly captures the surreal as well as the real effect of Sarah.

Noli me tangere Do not touch me. (Latin).

déshabille Partly dressed.

summonsed i.e. charged with.

a labour of Hercules The hero of Greek and Roman mythology who had to perform twelve labours. He was ranked among the gods.

tranced Absorbed, ecstatic.

but dallying with the wood-nymphs A superbly unconscious irony – for Charles had been dallying with Sarah.

Sodom and Gomorrah The ancient cities near the Dead Sea destroyed by fire from heaven because of their sinfulness (Genesis xviii–xix).

the enclosure acts A series of acts passed in the eighteenth century whereby common land had to be fenced and given ownership.

Anschluss Union (though particularly applied to the annexation of Austria by Germany).

de facto In fact.

draconian Based on the Athenian (seventh century BC) who established a severe code of laws, hence harsh, rigorous.

abbess Fine irony – she virtually keeps her servants in a nunnery.

the Victorian valley of the dolls Another modern image to make vividly present the effects of drug addiction.

as Coleridge once discovered ... presumably because he is supposed to have written *Kubla Khan* after an opium dream. Coleridge is the friend of Wordsworth, a romantic poet, fine critic (1772–1834).

Bosch-like picture from Hieronymus Bosch, outstandingly original Dutch painter (*c.*1460–1516).

the objective correlative A term coined by the modern poet T.S. Eliot (1888–1965) saying that the way to present emotion in a work of art is to provide 'a set of objects, a situation, a chain of events which shall be the formula of that *particular* emotion'.

like some pagan idol she looked ... Deliberate irony in view of the fact that she sees herself as being far from pagan.

I will not make her teeter ... Here Fowles is mocking Victorian melodrama and romance.

Chapter 13

The author now confronts the reader with his own methods, stressing the nature of his imagination, the fact that he is free to make his characters do what he wants (see notes below). This technique is much used by the major Victorian novelists (like Thackerary and George Eliot, for example), and this chapter opening is a cross between a parody of them and an engaging reminder to the reader that fiction is not reality. Fowles tells us that being free himself he has to confer freedom on his characters, and he admits, 'I do not fully control these creatures of my mind.' (page 87). There is even a joke with the reader that this is, after all, 'Chapter Thirteen'. Sarah goes on using Ware Commons, thus sealing her ultimate doom, while a superbly cynical image – 'a thunderous clash of two brontosauri' (page 88) signals a confrontation between Mrs Poulteney and her arch-enemy/ rival, Lady Cotton.

motto: Maud Isis was the nature goddess of Egyptian mythology.
Alain Robbe-Grillet and Roland Barthes The first the twentieth-century experimental French novelist, the second the French critic largely associated with the structuralist theory of criticism.
a novelist . . . has only to pull the right strings and his puppets will behave in a lifelike manner This is derived from Thackeray's famous remark at the end of *Vanity Fair* 'let us shut up the box and the puppets, for our play is played out'.
aleatory avant-garde Pioneering, innovatory,
I do not fully control these creatures of my mind i.e. they develop characteristics of their own. George Eliot once observed that sometimes her characters took her over, almost as if they had a life and independence of their own.
hypocrite lecteur Hypocritical reader, a quotation from the French poet Baudelaire (1821–67), author of 'Fleurs du Mal'.
In *The Waste Land* T.S. Eliot quotes the words at the close of Part I, hence their popular currency in the twentieth century.
a thunderous clash of two brontosauri The grotesque image – which is extended – shows how grotesque the two women are in their fanaticism.

Chapter 14

An ironic account of the boredom experienced by Charles two or three times a week as he has to go visiting in Lyme's social set-up. The day after the Undercliff incident Charles goes to Marlborough house. There is a neatly satirical parody of the gossipy conversation that occurs after such visits. During the visit the verbal fencing common among such disparate personalities takes place. The painting of Mrs Poulteney's dead husband (he died in

1851, the year of the Great Exhibition) is given some satirical treatment. Mrs Tranter's genuine warmth almost breaks through Sarah's conditioned reserve. Charles is on edge but Sarah manages to withdraw from all conversation. Of course there is a delicious sense here of the reader sharing the secret about which the others know nothing. Charles has the perspicacity to realize that Sarah is acting. The upstairs/downstairs interaction continues, with Mrs Poulteney's insulting interference over the question of Mary seeing Sam. It is there too after the secret look has passed between Sarah and Charles, for the author tells us that the conversation in the kitchen was much more serious than that pretentious religiosity which Mrs Poulteney has commanded in her drawing-room.

motto: Persuasion The quotation is from Chapter XVI. It fits neatly into this chapter, which has as its basis the required social visit and the attendant superficiality.

Periclean oration Derived from Pericles (495–429 bc), Athenian statesman and military commander responsible for raising the power of Athens.

the reginal hand Excellent adjectival irony – queenly.

icon Religious picture, the term here used ironically.

1851 Significantly, the year of the Great Exhibition.

Introit Psalm sung while the priest approaches the altar to celebrate Mass or Holy Communion.

That computer in her heart . . . See note page 26.

*Perhaps, in fairness to the lady . . . Fowles sometimes inserts, as here, a footnote to his own writing. Usually they are informative, but this one seems pretentious and heavy-handed in its jocularity.

Chapter 15

Ernestina's sensitivity because Charles has been snubbed by the revolting Mrs Poulteney causes her to behave passionately towards him when they reach home. After a while they see the humour of the situation. Charles now tries his particular brand of teasing interrogation on Sam in order to gauge the seriousness of Sam's intentions with regard to Mary. The conversation between Charles and Sam does not ring completely true, mainly because there seems to be a distortion of Sam's cockney dialect and Charles's wit is rather too heavy-handed. He also plays the moral mentor, telling Sam that he will not have Mary trifled with. Sam reveals that he is deeply in love with Mary. Again we are aware of the deliberate upstairs/downstairs interaction, and in view of Charles's secret over Sarah, we are inclined to think that the servants know their own minds better than their employers know theirs.

had been on hot coals outside i.e. waiting with nervous apprehension.
if her God was watching, He must have wished ... i.e. he would have been tempted by Mary's sexuality. The observation is typically Victorian in its authorial perspective, although here it is parody.
higgerance Ignorance.
Ursa Bear. (Latin)
a bargee's tool of trade i.e. the bargepole (with which Sam said he wouldn't touch Mary).
primum mobile Prime source or motion or action (Latin).
a certain past cynicism had come to roost i.e. Sam's past has caught up with him – ironic now that he is serious.
harms Arms.

Chapter 16

Careful chronology again, with Charles being occupied for five days with all the importance of small-talk and visits. Ernestina is already assuming the posture of the deferential wife. Charles finds this somewhat cloying, the long periods of boring time are dwelt on, and then the actual historical period is set once again, this time with reference to Mrs Norton's best-selling poem. The emphasis is an interesting one, since Mrs Norton (Melbourne's mistress?) occupies the same kind of anomalous social position as Sarah. The influence of the poem on Ernestina is described, together with its obvious 'eulogy of Florence Nightingale' (page 101). All this is carefully linked to John Stuart Mill's bill to give emancipation to women, and Ernestina's unfeminist reaction. But Ernestina has the spirit to weave a line of her own into the poem ridiculing Charles. Charles's afternoon off means that he can pursue his own interests and go searching for flints. The motive is supposedly scientific, but in reality sexual: he wants to meet Sarah. They meet unexpectedly and the descriptions of Sarah are strongly sensual, her eyes unusual and compelling. Charles suspects that she has a deep personality, and is a little ashamed of almost appreciating it, mainly because the conditioning of the age has taught him to reject definite sensuality. Their being interrupted raises the tension, then Charles continues his proprietary interest in Sarah, even urging her to leave the district, some help being found for her through the kindness of Mrs Tranter. Charles is waffling, perhaps half aware of his attraction to Sarah. The chapter ends on a climax as she flees, having revealed that the French Lieutenant is married.

mottoes: Tennyson and A.H. Clough See section on *The Victorian Novel* pages 13–14.
de rigueur Required by etiquette.
Cupid ... Maid Marian For the first see note page 23. The second is the sweetheart of Robin Hood.
contretemps Disagreement.
Mrs Caroline Norton's (1808–1877) Information about her is given in the text. She had the distinction of being fictionalized by George Meredith in *Diana of the Crossways* (1885).
The Edinburgh Review The famous periodical which could make or mar reputations. It was founded in 1802.
Melbourne's mistress Lord Melbourne (1779–1848), Prime Minister 1834, 1835–41.
Florence Nightingale (1820–1910) Established nursing as a profession after the Crimean War (1854–6) during which she devoted all her energies to bringing efficient nursing to the wounded and dying.
Lady of the Lamp The nickname given to Florence Nightingale.
Westminster i.e. in Parliament.
John Stuart Mill (1806–73) Author of 'On Liberty' (1859).
Disraeli See note page 19.
Punch The humorous weekly founded in 1841.
'You've gone to sleep, you hateful mutton-bone! Ernestina is not without a certain facile ability, as she shows here. But the verse is so bad that it lends itself to parody.
the Gibson Girl ... The style of beauty popular in the Edwardian Age (1901–10).
Lavater (1741–1801) Swiss poet, theologian and student of physiognomy.
Madame Bovary This novel of adultery, tragic in conception, was published in 1857. It is the masterpiece of Gustave Flaubert (1821–80).

Chapter 17

An account of the Assembly rooms in Lyme and their reputation for people like Mrs Poulteney. It is a place of small-town fashionable gossip. Charles meanwhile in his own thoughts knows that he is becoming obsessed by the enigma that is Sarah. He also realizes that it is becoming increasingly difficult to tell

Ernestina, for he is aware that she is of a jealous nature. He begins to sum up Ernestina herself, seeing into her limitations, and although he cannot define it, he seems to recognise that Sarah symbolizes what he feels he has missed and is missing in life. A neat parallel is now drawn with the other young couple, Sam and Mary, very different but obviously greatly attracted to each other. An authorial aside deplores the pressures of life in the twentieth century compared with what they were then. Sam is overcome by Mary's innocence, which contrasts tellingly with his own flash world. Sam's ambitions are spelled out, and the dialogue between this pair of lovers has the merit of being devoid of artificiality – and it is not without homely wit.

motto: Hardy See section on *The Victorian Novel* etc. page 13.
Ramadan Ninth month of the Muslim year involving a thirty-day fast.
Balmoral boots i.e. laced shoes.
Handel and Bach The first George Frederick (1685–1759), German-born composer famous for the 'Messiah'. Settled in England in 1712. The second Johann Sebastian (1685–1750), celebrated German composer.
a Byron tamed See note page 19.
moue Pout.
in his bed and in his bank . . . and of course in his heart too Note the irony here which embraces sex, money and romance.
his fraction of Eve i.e. Mary.
Seven Dials Narrow squalid area of London.
The world is only too literally too much with us now A deliberate echo of Wordsworth's (1770–1850) sonnet beginning 'The World is too much with us, late and soon/Getting and spending, we lay waste our powers.'
its go i.e. its spirit, its sharpness.
a-cock i.e. sideways (what had put him out, discountenanced him).
Dessay I dare say.
Happen Perhaps.
Us izzen 'lowed We aren't allowed to look at a man unless we are (officially) courting.
'ee wuz You were.
'A demang, madymosselle' Until tomorrow, mademoiselle (Sam's cockney French).
the Roman sign of mercy Thumbs up.
as if to a passing bier i.e. acknowledging a funeral and showing respect.

Chapter 18

Another free afternoon for Charles who has a travel lust upon him and heads for Ware Commons. He determinedly investigates the Undercliff, but Sarah surprises him (we know that he wants to be surprised). The light, the loneliness of the scene, make the appearance she presents impressive. She gives him two '*Micraster* tests' (page 121). Again there is the strong suggestion of a sexual atmosphere between them, particularly when their fingers touch. She has obviously taken his earlier offer to heart, and wishes to make an appeal to him. Charles is determined to resist but cannot bring himself to do so. She can see clearly the risk of going to London – the irony is that she is to do just that later. There is a definite mystical moment between them, but Charles is overcome by her intelligent and telling articulation of her feelings and her accurate account of her situation. She has the confidence to treat him as an equal in terms of intellect, and he finds this disconcerting. Fowles's style is often speckled with analogies, and here Sarah is equated with Calypso. Charles is still horrified by the emotionalism of the scene, particularly when Sarah begins to narrate the past. She feels that she is mad – and that her only escape is confession to him. She wants to arrange to meet him again but Charles adopts the role of 'Alarmed Propriety' (page 127). He agrees to meet her, alarmed indeed at the commitment – and of course he cannot now bring himself to tell Ernestina. Sarah's real power, which cuts right across convention, has been clearly demonstrated in this chapter.

the Morea The Peloponnese, part of Greece south of the isthmus of Corinth.

polypody Varieties of ferns growing on moist rocks, walls and trees.

Echinocorys scutata This is described in the next sentence.

Micraster **tests** External coverings or shells.

Moments like modulations come in human relationships i.e. changes (as indicated afterwards, to a subjective state).

status quo The way things are.

Odysseus . . . Calypso The first the wandering hero of Homer's *Odyssey*; Calypso was a nymph who lived on the island of Ogygie on which Odysseus was shipwrecked. She delayed his departure for seven years.

Doric temples See note page 23.

as if habited in glass i.e. not real flesh and blood.

Chapter 19

The eccentric Dr Grogan is the immediate focus of attention. He breathes life into the chapter by the quality of his personality, he obviously enjoys shocking people. He too is treated ironically (his imagination fills in the gaps of what he doesn't know). Charles meanwhile observes his fiancée, and still finds her somewhat lacking in positive qualities. Later Charles and Grogan talk, but before that Charles becomes more aware of the division in himself. At first the conversation covers the political, moral, social and philosophical spectrum open to two intelligent men of the period. A lengthy authorial interruption, having all the advantages of hindsight, contributes to the debate. Charles wants to talk about 'poor Tragedy'. Grogan provides some clinical definitions of madness, and then blames Marlborough House for Sarah's present state. The interesting thing is that Grogan too, in his medical capacity, has tried to get Sarah to leave. Grogan's theory is that she has become addicted to her misery – 'Her sadness becomes her happiness' (page 136). He believes that if she is allowed to reveal her feelings to someone she will be cured. This has a great effect upon Charles, though Grogan also believes that Sarah does not want to be cured.

There follows a sudden and dramatically effective switch to Sarah's bedroom. The deprivations of Millie lead to an authorial indictment of the conditions of the labouring poor in Victorian England. The coming together of Sarah and Millie in their warmth and unsexuality is described effectively by the writer. The author's presence in this chapter is pervasive, and we are almost startled by a phrase like 'Genesis is a great lie' (page 140). Fowles is always careful though to document what he says by close reference to scientific discovery in the period. Interestingly, both Charles and Grogan are passionately committed Darwinians.

motto: Darwin – *naturally selected* The key phrase in the survival of the fittest theory.
eunuchistic Hibernian ability i.e. the Irish capacity to exert charm verbally but without physical commitment. The tone is ironic.
A dry little kestrel ... Superbly economical and vivid metaphor.
Heidelberg German university on the river Neckar.
comme il faut Socially impeccable.
a wiff of corollary nausea ... This feeling of disgust is to be more fully indulged later because of Sarah's overwhelming attraction.

souffrante Suffering.

Hoffmann's Tales E.T.A. Hoffmann (1776–1822), the German romantic writer of fantasies, chief among them *The Devil's Elixir*.

the late Prince Consort Prince Albert married Queen Victoria in 1840 and died in 1861.

nereids The sea-nymphs, daughters of Nereus.

Gregorian telescope The first reflecting telescope invented by James Gregory (1638–75).

'For astronomical purposes only, of course' Irony – obviously he wants to look at the girls bathing.

without the tyranny of specialization Fowles has strong views on a number of issues, this being one of them.

Virgil (70–19 BC) Roman poet, author of *The Aeneid*.

Bentham Jeremy Bentham (1748–1832): he believed in 'the pursuit of happiness of the greatest number'.

Parian Fine white marble obtained from Paros.

Voltaire (1694–1778) Philosopher, dramatist, witty sceptical views.

Chartist See note page 19.

bull i.e. false.

Reform Bills of the 1830s The First Reform Bill was passed in 1832.

Augustan humanity The period of literary eminence identified with eighteenth-century writers like Pope.

Burke Edmund (1729–97), orator and statesman.

Matthew Arnold See the section on *The Victorian Novel* page 14.

Bedlam The hospital of St Mary of Bethlehem (founded 1247) which later housed lunatics, hence Bedlam = madness.

jarvey Driver of Irish jaunting-car.

Her sadness becomes her happiness This economical statement is an attempt to define Sarah's state clinically.

referred to an island in Greece i.e. Lesbos, the home of the Greek poetess Sappho.

Dr Phillpotts (1778–1869) High Churchman, Bishop of Exeter, attacked Reform and the Oxford Movement.

George Morland ... Birket Foster The first (1763–1804) English animal and landscape painter; the second (1825–99) the water-colour artist, illustrator.

its Versailles A reference to the splendour of the French palace, particularly during the reign of Louis XIV up to 1715.

wells of loneliness Writing with hindsight, Fowles has deliberately used the phrase which echoes the title of the novel *The Well of Loneliness* (1928) by Radclyffe Hall which was sympathetic towards lesbianism. It was banned after a prosecution for obscenity.

Lyell Sir Charles Lyell, English geologist (1797–1875).

Ussher James Ussher, Irish prelate (1581–1656).

coinciding very nicely with reform elsewhere i.e. the Great Reform Bill of 1832, for example.

Genesis is a great lie ... Again we note the strength of the author's views.

Gosse Edmund Gosse (1849–1928) essayist and critic.
bas-bleus Bluestockings (intellectual women).
carbonari Members of a secret society.

Chapter 20

A poetic description of Sarah, the focus sharply on her, with her supplicatory offering of the test and Charles's conversation with Grogan fresh in his mind. Charles now feels that he has a duty to help Sarah. He continues to role-play, however, and she leads him directly and unselfconsciously to the 'secluded place' where they can talk. Charles is fascinated by her hair – another sexual emphasis. Sarah is reassured by his attention and tells her story. It is characterised by realism and directness. Her account of her life with the Talbots shows how – despite their kindness – she is deprived in the cultural and emotional sense, everything that goes with the make-up of a feeling, suffering woman. All Sarah's reflex actions in this chapter have a sexual significance. She goes on with the story, revealing what she came to see as the truth about Varguennes. She says that she gave herself to him, but this lie is to be fully exposed later, and here seems a deliberate attempt to shock Charles, to face him with a truth which she suspects he will find unpalatable. There is a dramatic and emotional intensity in Sarah's narrative which sets her apart just as she believes she herself is set apart by her actions, her education, her situation and her reputation. Charles, by a leap of his own sympathetic imagination and his as yet unacknowledged sexual desire for Sarah, lives through her sexual surrender as if he is the French Lieutenant. The author has recourse to the period, the art of the period, the contrast with twentieth-century views, in order to stress the effect of Sarah's confession on Charles.

motto: William Manchester The reference is to the assassination of John Fitzgerald Kennedy in 1963. It is an oblique way of indicating Sarah's 'remarkable' quality through a modern reference.
a lady would have mounted behind ... The implication is that the lady's modesty would have been false.
al fresco In the open air, hence, exposed.
demi-monde Women of doubtful reputation, not accepted by conventional society.
microscopic cherubs' genitals ... defoliate the milkwort These are apparently casual sexual references which somehow reflect Sarah's intense sexuality.

the Unionists i.e. trades unionists.

So that they should know I have suffered . . . Sarah's intensity is both personal and symbolic. In extramarital sexual relationships in the Victorian period the woman, to use Hardy's words, pays.

Pre-Raphaelite The group of young artists and men of letters who were dedicated to impose the standards of art and literature which operated in the period before the great Italian artist Raphael (1483–1520).The leaders of the group were D. G. Rossetti, Millais, Holman Hunt and others from 1848 onwards.

Millais John Everett Millais (1829–96), perhaps the most celebrated of the Pre-Raphaelite painters.

Ford Madox Brown (1821–1893) Painter.

Constable John Constable (1776–1837) the celebrated landscape painter known particularly for 'The Hay Wain'.

Palmer (1805–81) English landscape painter.

Avila The Spanish town which was the birthplace of St Teresa.

Revision questions on Chapters 11–20

1 Consider the parts played by Mary and Sam in the narrative of these chapters.

2 Write an account of the most dramatic scene in these chapters, bringing out its particular qualities.

3 Compare and contrast any scene that Charles has with Ernestina with one he has with Sarah.

4 Describe how Charles tries to resist the temptation of seeing Sarah. How far do you think he is fooling himself?

5 Write about either (a) Dr Grogan's part in the story so far or (b) Sarah's story of her relationship with Varguennes. What does it reveal about her?

Chapter 21

Sarah's sensitivity prevented her from telling the complete truth to Mrs Talbot about Varguennes because Mrs Talbot's own happiness had driven Sarah to do what she says she did. Charles feels humiliated by her response to him, almost as if she considers that he is too conventional to understand. He again presses her to leave, and we suspect the self-interest present in the request, since he finds her disturbing and he does not really know what to do. He sees now what he senses is the possibility of a relationship of which he has had no conception before. In promising her Mrs Tranter's money, Charles is also deliberately buying her silence. As they descend and hear the laughter we feel their tension as they at first believe that they have been seen or even overheard. There is some humour in the situation when they realise that Sam and Mary are seeking solitude like themselves. Again we are aware of the upstairs/downstairs interaction. Charles is embarrassed by what he sees for he, too, is with his lover, just like his servant Sam. The enigma of Sarah's smile almost invites intimacy but Charles as ever is cautious, not yet so conquered by her as to abandon discretion. He suggests that they never meet again, Mary runs from Sam, Sarah leaves him, and Charles is left with his own inadequate response to the extraordinary communion he has inwardly experienced.

motto: Arnold See section on *The Victorian Novel* etc. page 14.
a proximity like a nakedness Read this section carefully. It anticipates
  their later coming together.
cozened – homilized Beguiled into – talked into.
in flagrante delicto In the very act of committing an offence (Latin).
viridian Yellowish-green colour.

Chapter 22

Charles is really in a self-congratulatory state, feeling that he has played with fire (his image) but not been seriously burned. Free will is now his touchstone – so he believes – and the authorial irony explores this. Locked in his time, Charles cannot see that Sarah has both passion and imagination. At this juncture there is the drama of Charles's uncle's telegram, which enables him conveniently to change direction in more senses than one. There is necessary retrospect on Ernestina's earlier visit to Winsyatt – it almost emphasises the gap between herself and Charles. A neat irony plays over what Charles thinks he has been summoned for and the truth which is so shortly to be revealed. The conversation between the lovers proves to be totally irrelevant in the light of Charles's uncle's coming marriage, which is revealed in the next chapter.

motto: Arnold See the section on *The Victorian Novel* etc. page 14.
had not been visited on him i.e. he had not suffered, been punished.

had not been visited on him i.e. he had not suffered, been punished.

the great stone claw of the Cobb Note the vividly personifying effect of the image.

but mint sauce to the wholesome lamb The commonplace food image is used by Charles but shows just how deluded he is by what has happened.

the fastest trap i.e. the quickest carriage.

Carolean i.e. Caroline, belonging to the period of Charles I and Charles II (roughly 1625–1649, and then 1660–85).

Tudor The period from 1485 to Elizabeth's death in 1603.

Gobelins Made at the state-run tapestry furniture factory of Gobelins in Paris, dating back to 1667.

Claudes Claude Lorraine (1600–82) landscape painter.

Tintoretto (1518–94) The Venetian painter.

Crystal Palace The original of iron and glass was built for the Great Exhibition of 1851, then moved to Sydenham. Ironically (in view of the remark here) it was accidentally burned down in 1936.

Chapter 23

The importance of Mrs Hawkins as surrogate mother to Charles in his childhood is given. There is a fine sense of period atmosphere, heightened by the social contrast of the workman and Charles's seigneurial assumption. The atmosphere aptly fits Charles's mood before the revelation – 'green todays flowed into green tomorrows' (page 171). Again a modern reference underpins the contrast between then and now, with social injustice given a stress-mark. The elimination of the bustard is a register of Charles's new position, and the structural coherence of the narrative is given a deliberate, fateful unity – Sarah's situation is about to be changed too. She has been seen by Mrs Fairley, and this will of course provoke the crisis. She has broken the rules imposed by Mrs Poulteney.

calash Here, a folding hood.

Carson's Stand From Kit Carson (1809–68), American trapper and scout.

Ramillies Scene of Marlborough's victory over the French (1706).

the Muses' Grove In Greek mythology, on Mount Olympus.

billycock Low-crowned hard felt hat.

landau Carriage.

green todays flowed into green tomorrows ... Lovely linking of colour with freshness and hope – rather like Andrew Marvell's lines from *The Garden*: 'Annihilating all that's made/To a green thought in a green shade.'

as vile as those taking place in Manchester and Sheffield ... Fowles' tone is again critical. See Mrs Gaskell's *Mary Barton* (1848) for insights into Manchester poverty.

And the motives... A further underlining of the attack on capitalism and what it leads to.

a Palladian structure Derived from the architectural style of the Italian architect Palladio (1508–80).

the younger Wyatt Probably Sir Matthew Digby Wyatt (1820–1877).

The immortal bustard had been banished Symbolic of Charles's own banishment from what he (and Ernestina) had come to regard as his inheritance.

Chapter 24

Note the immediacy of this chapter; the switch into direct dialogue-discussion of what the reader does not yet know has happened is particularly effective in raising the reader's expectations. Ernerstina's reactions are irrational (compare her with Sarah) and expose her limitations. She takes the uncle's decisions personally. Charles is now aware of her lack of breeding too, but all is subsumed by the dramatic announcement that Mrs Poulteney has dismissed Sarah. Two crises in a day for Charles! The fear is that Sarah has committed suicide. Charles is hypocritical enough to continue the deception, and even fears that Sarah has been seen with him, which would reveal all. He loses himself in action, the chapter ending with his setting off for the White Lion, where Sarah had sent her bags. Note that we have not been told (a) what happened at Winsyatt and (b) what happened between Mrs Poulteney and Sarah. Though we can guess both, the promised detailed explanation arouses the reader's excitement.

'Mrs Poulteney has dismissed Miss Woodruff' The bluntness of the announcement is equivalent to the physical shock it produces in Charles.

Chapter 25

On his arrival Charles reads the dramatic note from Sarah; his small-mindedness is shown by the fact that he feels she has risked his reputation by writing thus. The interreaction with Sam over the delivery of the note is an important plot point, for Sam is to put this and other events to his own use. Here Charles has to bind Sam to silence. The note she sends is in governess French. Charles's exclamation seems to betoken his jealousy of

Varguennes. Whatever it is, the tension is immediate. Charles leaves and Sam has gained useful information to manipulate his master with.

In a vivid insight . . . Time was the great fallacy This shows Charles's capacity for experience, thinking and feeling experience, and it also shows that he has the potential to transcend time and its conventions. This in part is what the novel is about.

'Je vous ai attendu toute la journée . . . après la ferme.' 'I have been waiting for you all day. I pray you – a woman on her knees asks you to help her in her anguish. I will spend the night in prayer for your coming. After dawn, I shall be at the little barn near the sea reached by the first footpath to the left after the farm.'

gasolier Gas light.

cobbler Strong drink of wine.

Inverness cape Cloak with removable cape.

Chapter 26

The exploration of Sam's dreams, about his future occupation and of Mary's place in it. Sam needs money, and the author now wordplays on mal and mail as a prelude to the way Sam's mind is working. The upstairs/downstairs interaction occurs at Winsyatt as well, and this leads naturally to what we have been expecting, the story of Charles's visit to his uncle. The uncle reveals his coming marriage: Charles is inwardly in turmoil but outwardly takes it well. There is some verbal fencing, but each knows what the other feels and the level of hypocrisy involved. Irony plays over the whole interchange, especially when Charles's uncle shows him a brood mare, an acquisition almost equated with that of the new wife. Charles feels depressed afterwards, almost with a feeling of inferiority towards Ernestina now that his inheritance has been (relatively) cut.

samovar A Russian tea-urn.

Piccadilly's . . . All types of collar.

the return golden shower Money.

Short-of-the-ready i.e. having no money.

a swell Man of fashion, having social status.

in the ring at Newmarket i.e. where the racehorses parade.

the frivolous grasshopper and his come-uppance i.e. they feel that Charles has merited his loss of inheritance.

imprimatur – or _ducatur in matrimonium_ Seal of marriage.

faute de mieux For want of a better.

niminy-piminy Mincing, prim.
Joe Manton (1766?–1835) Gunmaker of some fame who finally went
  bankrupt.

Chapter 27

Satirical opening here – Charles visiting Grogan – about sexual
practice and ignorance in the Victorian period. Charles plunges
into a nearly true confession to Grogan of his meetings with
Sarah – holding back the involvement of his own feelings, however. A letter of deception indicating that Sarah is safe – which
they don't know – is written. Grogan then undertakes to explain
Sarah psychologically, knowingly involving Charles and his feelings as he does so. He suggests that Sarah has deliberately
courted trouble in being seen by Mrs Fairley and has thus
precipitated her own crisis. Grogan then proceeds to analyse
Charles's situation with Ernestina. Charles confesses that he
feels possessed by Sarah, and Grogan explains to him what he
thinks Sarah feels for him (Charles). Charles is in fact desperate
to get Sarah out of his life. An asylum – an enlightened one – is
discussed, to Charles's great relief. The closing of the chapter
sees Charles in possession of the case history of Sarah which
Grogan has given him.

motto: A. H. Clough See *The Victorian Novel* page 14.
neither begotten nor born through the navel Indicates the degree of
  sexual ignorance in the Victorian period.
as if swearing on a Bible Very ironic in view of the fact that for many
  people, he being symbolic of them, the new Bible had become *The
  Origin of Species*.
in extremis ... de profundis ... de altis At the end ... from the
  depths ... from the heights (Latin).
a cholera, a typhus of the intellectual faculties Note the
  appropriateness of the image in view of the incidence of these diseases
  in Victorian England.
What did Socrates die for? Socrates (469–99 BC) condemned to death
  for corrupting the young.
Malthus Thomas Malthus (1766–1835). He was the clergyman who
  wrote a celebrated essay on Population, urging that increase of
  population should be stopped by employing sexual restraint.
Homo sapiens Man, as distinct from animals.
like a man possessed Since Charles has been urged to know himself,
  this is rightly defining what he feels with regard to Sarah.

Chapter 28

This effectively is a break with the direct narrative. It is an illustrative story within a story. The La Roncière accusations and trial form an interesting comment on deception, corruption, the inadequacy of French law and the psychological and sexual states of Marie and Miss Allen. In effect it is also an analysis of the effects of the menstrual cycle, given through a number of examples which are particularly powerful for the extremes to which the person concerned has gone. Charles is greatly moved and upset by what they reveal. Undoubtedly Grogan intends that they should reveal to him the hysteria from which Sarah is, supposedly, suffering. Charles finds it difficult to apply the cold light of scientific reason to the stories.

mottoes: Clough and Arnold See the section on *The Victorian Novel* page 14.
the pernicious notions of freedom disseminated by the French Revolution i.e. liberty, equality, fraternity.
Bedlam See note page 38.
Sir Galahad . . . Guinevere The first the son of Lancelot, one of the Knights of the Round Table, notable for his purity and for his achievement in finding The Holy Grail. Guinevere was the wife of King Arthur but she fell in love with Lancelot – hence the ironic emphasis here.
Pontius Pilate The Roman Procurator of Judea who believed in Christ's innocence, yielded to those who wished to crucify him, but washed his hands to cleanse himself of any guilt for Christ's death.

Chapter 29

Early morning description of the scene with Charles leaving the White Lion. Vivid images accompany the description, many of them detailed, evocative, bright with the immediacy of the experience. An analogy with art is almost inevitable: here it has a strongly spiritual connotation. It is a poetic hymn to nature. Surrounded by all this, and certainly aware of a spiritual communion with the absent Sarah, Charles feels that he is being watched. He approaches a barn, pushes open the door, convinced that he will see Sarah. He doesn't but there is a slight sound. On that dramatic note the chapter ends.

St Hubert (656–728) Patron saint of huntsmen.
pseudo-Linnaean See note on Linnaeus page 25.
a numberless Greek chorus The chorus was an integral part of Greek
   tragedy, announcing, foretelling, commenting on, hence the force of
   the reference here.

Chapter 30

Retrospect on Sarah – what happened betweeen her and Mrs
Poulteney, the whole scene admirably prepared by Mrs Fairley.
The evil of the place and its practices are seen in the fact that
Mrs Fairley eavesdrops on the interview. The exchanges are
brief. Initially Sarah's silence rules, and she certainly rules at the
end when she chooses, after a succinct comment on the hypocrisy she has experienced at Marlborough House, to bring God
into the discussion. The reaction afterwards is extreme. Sarah
breaks down in the lonely privacy of her room, believing that she
is praying but in reality isolated, forlorn, an outcast in her own
mind as well as in practical fact.

verjuice The acid juice of crab-apples and grapes used in cooking.
Parthian shaft Normally 'Parthian shot', a reference to the fact that
   the Parthians shot arrows while they were retreating.
You wicked Jezebel! ...' The latter the wife of Ahab, synonymous with
   wickedness (see I Kings xxi 1–29 and 2 Kings ix 30, 37 for her death).

Revision questions on Chapters 21–30

1 How would you describe the development of the relationship
between Charles and Sarah in these chapters?

2 How does the author treat Charles's loss of Winsyatt? What
effect does it have on the story?

3 There are switches of time in the narrative. What effect does
this have on you, the reader? You might consider the delay, for
example, before we are actually told what happened between
Charles and his uncle.

4 Do you consider that Chapter 28 (the various factual histories
of female sexual hysteria) adds anything to the novel? Say clearly
what you feel about its inclusion.

5 Write about the atmosphere created by John Fowles in either

Charles's impetuous search for Sarah or in the scene between Mrs Poulteney and Sarah.

Chapter 31

Dramatic return to the barn – the reader's expectation has been aroused but left unsatisfied two chapters ago. Sarah is curled up asleep. Charles is drawn towards her sympathetically and sexually and, although he doesn't wish to, he speaks. When she moves Charles is on edge, fearing that the place is too open and that they may be discovered. When they begin to speak Charles is still intent on his protective and guiding role, telling her that she must leave Lyme. Her passionate response amazes him, takes him by surprise. Eventually, largely because he is unresponsive, she reveals that she has deliberately brought about the crisis with Mrs Poulteney. Charles realizes that she loves him, succumbs enough temporarily to kiss her, pushes her away, and rushes out to we know not what, so dramatically is this chapter organized.

motto: A. H. Clough Note the mixture of ecstasy and cynicism in this quotation from Clough.

a wildness of innocence, almost an eagerness Sarah is of course, at this stage, sexually innocent, despite what she has said.

existentialist moments Individual moments where there is a free and responsible exertion of the will.

Catullus (87–54? BC) Roman love poet celebrated for his epigrams too.

Sappho (about 610 BC) Greek poetess of Lesbos.

lachrymatory glands Tear ducts.

Chapter 32

Switch back to Ernestina and her belief on the previous night that Charles is displeased with her. She is also somewhat relieved not to be mistress of Winsyatt, since she prefers the easy life of being waited on rather than being in charge of everything and having to exert herself. This is followed by an authorial commentary on the nature of the middle-class. Ernestina has sufficient ostentation to sit up while Charles is out at night, so that her light will indicate she is awake (all is confided to her diary). In fact the record of her diary is a pathetic self-indictment, and a prayer to be good and obedient in marriage to Charles. Upstairs/

downstairs interaction continues with Sam's being given orders to be ready to leave at midday. Mary is upset, but there is some comedy when Sam has a heavy fall in the street trying to reach her.

chatelaine Mistress of the house, holding the keys etc.
Janus-like Janus was the Roman god of doors and gates, having two faces, one at the back and one at the front.
peignoir See note page 22.

Chapter 33

Back to the barn – and we are brought up to date again – this time discovering that as Charles left the barn Sam and Mary are coming towards it. Charles as always is mindful of his own reputation and seeks to bind Sam and Mary to silence. When the two latter leave they see the humour of the situation. Charles condescendingly takes blame for having engaged Sarah's affections, tells her that she is being sought and that she must leave Lyme (again), gives her money and takes leave of her. We feel his selfishness, his rejection of his own sexuality (and love) and we feel too the strength of her presence. Most positively of all we feel that Sarah is a much greater individual than Charles: his own word 'remarkable' does her only part credit. She is more than that, and much more than he can cope with.

Charles's hand came to a mumbling stop Note the effect of 'mumbling', indicative of indecision.
slombest hoath Solemnest oath.

Chapter 34

The exchange between Charles and Ernestina as a result of this (Ernestina not knowing what has happened) is stiff. Ernestina has suffered the further embarrassment of not being able to overhear what Charles has been saying to Aunt Tranter. Charles continues to lie, using the excuse that he must see Ernestina's father to tell him about the new state of affairs. The author continues to implement the period atmosphere, here with female fashion as the point of reference. Significantly, Charles does not kiss Ernestina on the mouth, an indication of the effect kissing Sarah has had subconsciously on him. But she forces him to it, and the result, to his own shame, is the awakening of sexual desire in him despite what has happened with Sarah. Charles feels it necessary to bribe Mary on the way out.

a sugar Aphrodite The Greek goddess of love identified with the Roman Venus.

the disgraceful Mrs Bloomer The latter (1818–94) who advocated sensible clothes for women, small jacket, skirt reaching just below the knee, trousers under this to the ankle.

Chapter 35

An authorial commentary on sexuality and repression in the nineteenth century, with special sections on prostitution, sanitation, pornography and social conditions generally. There is detail on birth control and the Victorian attitude to sex. This leads into some comments on the lack of innocence in the rustic workers (Mary is supposedly being kept in mind throughout) and then to Hardy and his breaking the 'Victorian middle-class seal over the supposed Pandora's box of sex' (page 235). Hardy's affair (if that is the right word) with his cousin Tryphena Sparks is then discussed, before returning to Mary, who obviously knows much more than her mistress about sexual sin. We note that the story has not moved forward. Fowles is using the Victorian omniscient author's technique. This commentary, by keeping the narrative in the background, has built up suspense about what actually **is** happening.

motto: Children's Employment Commission Report This factual report is a striking indictment of the enforced (so to speak) immorality among the Victorian agricultural class. One gets the impression that in the overcrowded cities it was even worse.

Dr Bowdler Thomas Bowdler (1754–1825) whose edition of Shakespeare (1818) cut out all references of a sexual nature so that the plays could be used as family reading without offence.

the strict threshold of the age i.e. when Victoria came to the throne (1837).

Malthus See note page 45.

Mayhew Henry Mayhew (1812–87), first editor of *Punch*, but famous for his *London Labour and the London Poor* (1851), a major sociological and moral investigation of the working class in all its deprivation in London.

Pandora's box of sex In Greek mythology Pandora (all gifted) had her box broken open, with all its evils scattered. Only Hope remained in the box.

Edmund Gosse's See note page 39.

Atreids ... Mycenae The first, the descendants of Atreus, were capable of many crimes: the second, Agamemnon's kingdom, celebrated for its archeological findings.

Tolpuddle Martyrdom The six farm labourers from the Dorset village who were sentenced to transportation in 1834 for trying to form a union. Their sentences were remitted in 1836: their stand marks the effective beginning of Trades Unionism.

Egdon Heath Features in Hardy's novels, notably *The Return of the Native*, (1878).

Jude the Obscure (1895) After this novel Hardy virtually turned his back on fiction and returned to his first love, poetry.

Chapter 36

Exeter a hundred years ago, the Endicott Family Hotel, with a fictional camera tracking the scene for the readers of today. Sarah's arrival and the small treats she has indulged herself show how deprived she has been in the past – and is now. Somewhat annoying authorial comments continue to clog the narrative. There is sensuality in the description of the way she holds the nightgown, mystery in the roll of bandage (though look ahead to what happens). The main pathos of the chapter indicates that she is indeed making the stay here a holiday, the only one she has ever had. Like all holidays, the days of this one are numbered.

a red light quarter i.e. the brothel area.

Charles Wesley (1707–88) Methodist, brother of the founder of Methodism, John: author of many hymns.

the first truly feminine gesture I have permitted her Note the authorial determination to remind us of his control and to stress too that we are merely reading fiction.

Chapter 37

Introduction to the character of Mr Freeman, his religiosity, his business ability and his suspicion of Charles, or at least of Charles's motives in coming to see him. Again we are aware of the polite verbal fencing that is going on. As Charles looks out of the window at the shopgirl and the soldier we feel that this simplicity of love is what he is lacking. He is also played upon by his prospective father-in-law, who senses that Charles is a snob and that he will not wish to be associated with trade. Charles cannot bring himself to say this, and although he is totally unsuited for what is being suggested, he promises to give it thought. At this stage he cannot transcend the conventions and prejudices of his own time.

like Mr Jorrocks The famous hunting character who features in books by the Victorian novelist R. S. Surtees (1805–64).
homologue Corresponding.
a nice patina of philanthropy A neatly turned phrase, as smooth as the activity described.
Marcus Aurelius Marcus Aurelius Antoninus (121–180) Stoic philosopher, Roman Emperor, author of meditations.
Lord Palmerston (1784–1865) Prime Minister 1855–8, 1859–65.
unlike the more famous pilgrim i.e. Christian, in John Bunyan's (1628–88) *Pilgrim's Progress*.
savoir-vivre Good breeding.

Chapter 38

We are given the immediate perspective of the Second Reform Bill, passed in 1867, the year of all this significant fictional action. Charles walks the streets, aware of his rank and status, aware too of the social differences he sees all around him. The atmosphere of the period is authentically captured. Contrast plays an effective part in the description, while Charles becomes more and more dissatisfied with himself, seeing that he feels that his father-in-law to be despises him. He feels that he has been purchased to serve a purpose – to give Ernestina rank – but that he will have to pay for it himself by demeaning himself. Strangely he comes across Freeman's store in Oxford Street, and this confirms his feelings and his wish to escape from them. He cannot bear the thought of participating, in the upper reaches even, of what we would call the rat-race. His reactions are neatly summarized by the author as an attempt to preserve his identity. He is imprisoned in the standards and demands of his period.

Hyde Park . . . three weeks later There were riots in Hyde Park in 1867, which saw the passing of the Second Reform Bill.
Candide From the satire by Voltaire (1694–1778).
saurian Like a lizard.
fusees Large-headed matches.

square pill-boxes i.e. hats.
an image-boy i.e. seller of pictures, prints.
curried i.e. rubbed down.
curlicues Decorative curls or twists.
nouveau riche i.e. newly-rich people.
behemoth See Job xl:15: an enormous creature.
Darwin or a Dickens For the first see note page 19. Dickens (1812–70), the great nineteenth-century novelist who voiced his disapproval of so much social injustice in a number of novels beginning with *Pickwick Papers* (1835–6).
preux chevaliers Gallant knights.

Chapter 39

The club visit by Charles, his companions seen satirically but with some understanding and the good points brought out. Nevertheless, this is a study in Victorian high-life debauchery. Society slang and feeble punning precede it, with Charles unable to take the liquor and remain steady which his companions are used to. In his semi-drunken state he sees what the trip to Ma Terpsichore's is about, and explains his own need to himself: after Sarah and the closer contact with Ernestina (in the physical sense) he needs a woman. The account of the journey, the area of London, 'the great whores' (page 262) are all redolent of the genuine atmosphere. An authorial lecture establishes the continuity of the sexual practices described in this chapter, linking the Victorian era with our own day and age. Charles goes, but sees his companions for what they are and is sexually excited as well as revolted. His sudden leaving is with the best of intentions, his moral stance – duty, his engagement vows to Ernestina – clearly in his mind. He picks up a prostitute whose initial appearance reminds him of Sarah. She reads his mind, for Charles, always cautious, fears that he may contract venereal disease from her. She reassures him before he can speak though, knowing Charles, he probably wouldn't have spoken anyway.

Mytton John (1796–1834) Sportsman and eccentric who spent a fortune and died in the King's Bench prison.
Casanova (1725–98) The Italian whose memoirs describe his multiple love affairs.
green Innocent, inexperienced.
Demmed Damned.
'discuss' i.e. eat and drink.

Ma Terpsichore's She was the muse of lyric poetry and dance in Greek mythology. The tone here is ironic.

Metonymia Substitution of the name or attribute for the thing meant – the shrine of love (Venus) for *puella* (girl).

cigar 'divans' Cigar shops, or smoking rooms attached to one.

penny-gaffs Low theatres and music-halls.

'weed' Cigar or cigarette.

Camargo French or Mexican.

Heliogabalus Roman Emperor (AD 218–22) noted for profligate behaviour and silliness.

Agamemnon Leader of the Greek forces besieging Troy: murdered by his wife Clytemnestra on his return home.

Cleland John (1709–89), his masterpiece *Fanny Hill* named here.

Bagnio Brothel.

A Covey of Town Partridges i.e. men about town, loose livers.

Chapter 40

Note Charles's sensitivity with regard to the cab-driver, who is invested with a silently critical view of him, so he feels. There is a detailed description of the prostitute's room, which acts as effective contrast both to Charles's background and the obscene representations at Ma Terpsichore's. The conversation does not ring true, though there is a convincing atmosphere. Despite the mechanistic approach of the girl, there is considerable sexuality in the scene. All the while we are aware of Charles's battle with himself, or rather with his stomach. The ending of the chapter is superb. When she tells him her name his non-sexual climax arrives with all the sudden anguish of nausea, both physical and emotional. This, of course, is what his Sarah could so easily become, despite all her uniqueness, when she finds that she has to support herself.

an Etty nude By William Etty, celebrated nineteenth-century painter (1787–1849).

the Pygmalion myth Pygmalion, King of Cyprus, fell in love with the statue he had created. Aphrodite breathed life into it.

Revision questions on Chapters 31–40

1 Write an essay on one incident in these chapters which seems to you to be unexpected, bringing out the effects which are produced.

2 Write an essay explaining what Charles thinks are his motives with regard to Sarah.

3 Chapter 35 has little to do with the narrative. What has it told you about the Victorians and about Hardy in particular that you didn't know?

4 Compare and contrast Sarah's experience in the hotel with Charles's experience in his interview with Mr Freeman.

5 Give an account of Charles's London experiences, bringing out his reactions as they occur.

Chapter 41

We are now used to the sudden switches in narrative, and here we are taken to Charles's unpremeditated return at midnight. Retrospect is now employed to describe the previous night after the vomiting. This Sarah proves to be both warm and practical, first helping Charles and then departing to get a cab. Charles is left literally holding the baby, a new and somewhat chastening experience for him. He contemplates the strangeness of the situation – 'the end of his great debauch' (page 278). He ponders on time. With the return of the girl he is moved again to the reflex humanity which his money makes possible.

motto: Tennyson See the section on *The Victorian Novel* etc. page 13.
sartin Certain.
lall Coo.
brougham Carriage.
the Sartrean experience Derived from Jean-Paul Sartre (1905–80), major French writer and philosopher of existentialism.

Chapter 42

Charles has the decency to apologise to Sam for his rudeness of the previous night. As usual Charles thinks about himself and his role both in the previous night's experiences and in his future with Ernestina. Then he deals with the letter from Grogan, provoked by his own letter, but which gives news of Sarah's presumed departure for Exeter. It also warns Charles that she may follow him to London. The next 'letter' contains merely three words – an address. Charles's announcement that he is going back to Lyme provokes Sam into confessing that he is going to marry Mary, and also that he wants – remember that Charles has been invited into trade too – to set up as a shop-keeper. Charles does not welcome change, Sam acts injured when his ideas are rejected and hypocritically when he 'learns' of Charles's uncle's marriage. Charles does think things over though, and decides he may speak to Mr Freeman on Sam's behalf later. Sam has got everything worked out. Charles's marriage would perhaps give him the money he needs, but he might also get it through a little discreet blackmail over Charles and Sarah.

éclairissement Enlightenment.
à la lettre In writing.
Absolvitur Absolution.
hask for 'er 'and Propose to her.
merrid Married.
hower Hour.
some of the ready See note page 44.
heekomonies Economies.
penchant Taste, liking for.
twigged Understood.
reproskitated Reciprocated, returned.
Hope Abandoned This comment refers to Sam's exaggerated pose in reaction to what has been said.
the whipped dog See previous note.
ante **Stanislavski** Before the advent of Stanislavski, the celebrated Russian dramatic producer (1865–1938).
Uriah Heep The crawling subservient blackmailing hypocrite of Dickens' *David Copperfield* (1848–50).
escritoire Writing-desk.
the uncouth Yankees descended to telegraphese The telegraphic cable was completed in July 1866, another casual reference which shows the author's attention to chronology.

Chapter 43

Charles interprets what has happened in his own way, feeling that the incident with the one Sarah – the prostitute – has put him on the right track now, and that he will marry Ernestina. He feels however that it would be a betrayal of the real Sarah to have her put into an institution. He goes to Exeter on his way to Lyme. Then he falls asleep, perhaps as a refuge.

As for Sarah . . . the other Sarah The substance of this is that Charles
believes there is a danger that Sarah Woodruff will be forced to turn to
prostitution.
as mournfully as a tumbril The association is with the French
revolution, the tumbrils being the carts that conveyed victims to the
guillotine and their bodies from it.

Chapter 44

Arrived at the White Lion, Charles and Sam go through their
own forms of interaction with their respective mates. In
Charles's case there is some romantic interplay over the watch-
pocket and some obvious punning, followed by his present to
Ernestina. He begins his story of Sarah, and an unexpected
authorial interruption indicates that the novel has ceased.
Fowles then writes all the imaginary might-have-been endings,
following out the happy-ever-after tradition but also waxing
satirical over the entrance of Mrs Poulteney into Heaven, or
rather being consigned to Hell and attributing it to Lady Cotton.
This is obviously a private joke with the reader, who can now sit
back and enjoy seeing the characters given back their life from
now until the end (or ends!).

motto: A. H. Clough Note how relevant this is to the main concerns of
the novel. It applies particularly to Charles.
And so ends the story. What happened to Sarah, I do not know . . .
Once again this is the author having his private joke with the reader.
He is expressing impatience at having to go on with his narrative, but
at the same time he is indicating the other lives the characters might
have led. This is a part of the best Victorian fiction, present in George
Eliot and Hardy.
barouche See note page 26.
as in ancient Egypt A reference to the practice of complete burial of
the household.
Jubilate Hymn of joy.
a much more tropical abode Hell.

Chapter 45

We learn that what we have just read happened in fact in
Charles's imagination, that the author has gone along with an
ending which does not in fact happen. Charles was really – as we
might expect in all consistency – tormented by Sarah's brief
letter. Now we learn what really happened when the train

stopped at Exter – Charles orders Sam to see that they are put up at the Ship hotel. Sam finds out about Endicott's Family Hotel, and then, after being dropped by the cabby, proceeds to spy on Charles, who goes to Endicott's Hotel. The compulsion of Sarah's attraction has drawn him there.

the last few pages you have read are not what happened See note about the authorial comment in the previous chapter.
oxymoron Figure of speech in which apparent contradictions are used to convey the truth.
the Delphic From the Oracle of Delphi, whose responses were ambiguous, riddles.
dolly me up Take me.
a couple o' browns Two pennies.

Chapter 46

Charles's enquiry brings forth news of Sarah's 'accident'. Even at this stage he vacillates, thinking he ought not to see her. She seems more vulnerable because of her 'accident'. She also seems ashamed, and we wonder if the 'accident' might have been deliberate. As he looks at her, Charles now knows why he has come – he had to see her, and the commonplace image of thirst is used to convey the extremity of his need. The two naked nymphs are almost an invitation, reminding the reader in their muted way of the more suggestive representations at Ma Terpsichore's. Sarah's tears rather than the nymphs stir his lust. There follows a finely judged description of their coming together – poetic, vital, sexual, inevitable. The prose is urgent with his need and action, and even contains a subtly comic element in Charles's manic undressing. Sarah is virtually passive but acquiescent, a few caresses apart. Yet when we have read it we feel the tremendous immediacy of the writing.

two naked marble nymphs above the fireplace Note how the irony is present here, with the strange reminiscence of the unbridled sexuality of Ma Terpsichore's.
Syncopal i.e. feeling faint.

Chapter 47

Charles is horrified by what he has done, and an atomic analogy shows the author's own hindsight about the fictional event.

Sarah's acute class awareness shows itself, but she appears to be telling Charles that he should leave her, that she will make no demands on him. She bewilders Charles by her capacity to sacrifice for love. His natural reaction is to feel the inadequacy of his own sex and the fact that he and Grogan have misjudged her. The author's implication is that Charles, like most Victorian males, cannot believe that a woman is capable of any full sexual enjoyment. The result is that here he feels that he has abused her. When he comes to the knowledge that Sarah is a virgin and that she has lied over Varguennes, he thinks that she has done all this in order to gain a hold over him, to blackmail him. She reappears to tell him the truth (the truth?) about what happened when she went to Weymouth to see Varguennes, and he notices that now she walks without a limp. She insists that her love for Charles is sincere, but cannot explain her other act of deception. Sarah is certainly an enigma. She reiterates that he cannot marry her.

was like a city . . . atom bomb Note again the force of the modern image.
succubi Female demons supposed to have sexual intercourse with men in their sleep.

Chapter 48

Charles's night-walks here take a new turn, that of entering a church for sanctuary. He is overcome when he realizes the inadequacy of his prayers, breaks down into weeping, seeing Sarah's face where he had hoped to see Christ's. Fowles follows this with a lecture on the Victorian concept of Christ, and afterwards a dialogue between the two selves of Charles. Perhaps most impressive of all in view of Charles's own deceptions is the idea that 'Duty is but a pot' (page 313). He comes ultimately to a transcendent view of Christianity, seeing in Christ 'the smiling peace of a victory brought about by, and in, living men and women' (page 315). He feels the presence of the dead around him. The author interposes some lines from Tennyson's *In Memoriam* in order to demonstrate how the dead rule the living, who constantly have their eyes on the past rather than on the future. Charles feels that Christ must be 'uncrucified' in order to be understood. The experience is profoundly personal, mystical.

motto: Tennyson Note that this is a comment on Charles by indicating his capacity to put the past behind him and become a new man.

Mater Dolorosa by Grünewald The celebrated seventeenth-century
 painter of religious scenes – the suffering mother being the Virgin
 Mary.

Bradlaugh Charles Bradlaugh (1833–91), the social reformer.

Where shall I begin?/Begin with what you have done ... This
 sequence is not dissimilar to the question and answer sequence in
 James Joyce's *Ulysses* (1922).

I do but render unto Caesar ... See Matthew xxii:21.

These nails you hammer through my palms? The direct association is
 with the Crucifixion.

rictus Gaping mouth.

Do we indeed desire the dead ... *In Memoriam* is so important to a full
 understanding of *The French Lieutenant's Woman* that the interested
 student is recommended to read it.

St Paul on the road to Damascus See Acts ix:1–22.

Uffizi Gallery in Florence.

Chapter 49

The irony is that when Charles sees the clergyman again he
realises that the young man represents the ostentation of the
High Church practice of the period. Charles is still held by
conventions but now comes to realise why Sarah has deceived
him – the whole series of deceptions has been to 'unblind' him.
There follows an authorial analysis of Victorian schizophrenia in
order to explain Charles's, and to explain further the divisions
between the body and the soul. Charles tries to expiate guilt on a
practical level by washing his bloody nightshirt. He then further
indulges his guilt by writing Sarah a love letter in which he says,
rather pompously, that he is going to break his engagement. He
seems unaware, except in passing, that this committing himself
to paper is leaving himself open to that self-interested predator,
Sam. The episode of the brooch seems grotesque and insensi-
tive, that of the dialogue between Sam and Mary an indication
that Sam knows what his master is up to and that he will outdo
him whatever happens.

en passage Passing through.

the Tractarian schism i.e. the Oxford Movement – the Tracts for the
 times – which effectively separated the Church of England into High
 and Low Church.

Tennyson, Clough, Arnold, Hardy ... See the section on *The Victorian
 Novel*.

Charles Kingsley (1819–75) Novelist, poet, clergyman.

detritus Matter, what is washed away.

Dr Jekyll and Mr Hyde R. L. Stevenson's masterpiece on the effect of drugs in splitting the personality was published in 1886.

Gothick Gothic novels – novels of horror, the supernatural, mystery and romance, flourished from 1760–1830.

anabatic epistle Passionate letter.

Chapter 50

This long chapter (long by Fowles's standards) is the confrontation scene between Charles and Ernestina. We notice that by a strange irony Charles uses the word Sarah used to define her inadequacy to him – 'unworthy'. There is also the irony that the loving telegram was sent before he had made love to Sarah. Ernestina finds it hard to accept Charles's assertion that he did not love her in the past. Her response to his lies is masterly – she believed that she would benefit from the marriage by pleasing him and becoming more complete. She only diminishes her case by referring to her diary, but her fluency, her passion, her self-truth, all reveal Ernestina to be much more than we – or Charles – thought she was. She has the intuition too to realise that something has happened and to confront Charles with it. Even Charles's confession is lying. Ernestina is reduced to counteraction. Revenge is going to be bitter. Mary cradling Ernestina's head makes a picture of retribution for Charles.

like October leaves Note the simple effectiveness of the image.
the catatonia of convention State of muscular rigidity and mental stupor – conventional because this is what is expected.

Revision questions on Chapters 41–50

1 Give an account of the precautions taken by Charles to keep his reputation intact.

2 Write about the authorial interventions to the narrative (including the fantasy about Mrs Poulteney). Say whether you find this irritating or not and why.

3 Write a critical account of the coming together of Charles and Sarah. Who do you think is the stronger character here and why?

4 Explain the roles played by Sam and Mary in these chapters.

5 Trace clearly the process by which Charles discovers and come to terms with himself.

6 Write a detailed account of the scene between Charles and Ernestina.

Chapter 51

This brief chapter has Charles making his explanations to Grogan who, he believes, has misjudged Sarah. Grogan is angry but, strange for an Irishman, not articulate (though duty calls him). After that Charles has to face Sam, who now knows via Mary what has happened. The result is that Sam gives notice, Charles is enraged (and humiliated) and nearly retracts (when Sam has gone) all that he did with Ernestina. This is the beginning of his suffering: dramatically, Grogan is announced.

motto: Arnold Notice that this is written some two years after the main action of the narrative.
Judas The betrayer of Christ.
Honly Only.

Chapter 52

The reaction of Aunt Tranter to the overwhelming news, and Grogan's anger at Charles's behaviour, both show how incapable they are of grasping anything that departs from the norm. To be fair to Grogan he is something of a psychiatrist, and knows that the best thing is to make as much of Ernestina as possible. He is confident that she will recover soon. He wants to know too why Mary is creating such a fuss. Mary gives her account to Aunt Tranter of the 'istricks' (page 337). Then she breaks down herself, but does not yet reveal everything to Aunt Tranter, though the latter enjoys the surrogate motherhood thrust upon her and promises to care for Mary until she gets married.

non sequitur It does not follow (Latin) = Illogical inference.
tooken by the istricks Taken with hysterics.
reffrums Reference.

Chapter 53

Now back to Grogan's entry upon Charles. Grogan proves to be intolerant of Charles's explanations and, more particularly, of his lies. Charles is adamant that there is no escaping the effects of self-knowledge. Grogan, however, is more bark than bite, and soon gets around to asking if Charles will marry Sarah. Charles replies in the affirmative, though he is really acting in the dark. Grogan is still suspicious though he realizes that now Charles is speaking the truth. He has a deep insight into Charles, knows that he is suffering, doubts him not a little, threatens him but is, overall, sympathetic.

Dante The great Italian poet Dante Alighieri (1265–1321), author of the philosophical poem *The Divine Comedy*.
Antinomians Those who believe that the moral law is not binding on Christians and that faith alone is sufficient for salvation.
commination Denunciation, threatening of divine punishment.
obfuscating cant Obscure hypocrisy.
Jacta alea est The die is cast.
your march away from the Rubicon Caesar crossed the Rubicon and thus committed himself to war against the Senate and Pompey. That implies decision, the phrase here implying the reverse.

Chapter 54

Not being able to find Sam (remember he has resigned) Charles sets off. Charles dreams of life with Sarah in London, but he is circumscribed by his own conventional views. There follows the shock when he arrives at Endicott's Hotel to find that Sarah has left for London, and there is worse to come. Sam did not leave the message or the package, so Sarah knows nothing of Charles's thoughts. His prayers now contrast markedly with his prayers of repentance after their coming together. He wants only to find her.

aboulia Loss of will-power.

Chapter 55

Charles's rail journey to London, with the uncomfortable passenger opposite threatening everything and doing nothing. Fowles has here captured one of the commonplaces of rail journeys – our ability to invest our fellow-travellers with thoughts and emotions of which they know nothing. At this point an authorial interruption underlines the temptation to leave Charles on the train and finish here; but once again the author acknowledges his responsibilities to Victorian fiction, and realizes that he must write on if he is to observe the convention. The passenger is the author; he disappears, and his character is free to develop to the end.

the Gorgon stare The gorgons were three sisters in Greek mythology whose stares turned those who looked directly at them to stone.
Spurgeon Charles (1834–92) widely known Baptist preacher.
douce Sweet.
But the conventions of Victorian fiction . . . Always these are at Fowles's elbow, and he gives his views here.

Chapter 56

Charles and the search via his private detectives (again documented to provide period authenticity). Through his own searches and experiences Charles comes to understand why there is reason for Sarah's resentment at her lot – and the lot of so many women – in the society of the time. Meanwhile the legal redress which the Freemans require gets under way. With a top counsel, who is brilliantly unpleasant, against him, Charles is now beginning to suffer another kind of experience. The document of his guilt which he has to sign humiliates him completely. He knows now that he will be further exposed if he tries to marry, and that he owes what freedom he has to Ernestina.

columbarium This was an underground sepulchre with incinerating urns.
vulpine Foxlike, crafty, cunning.
basilisk quiz The fabulous reptile which killed by a look, hence the comparison here.
sine die Adjourned indefinitely.
prima facie Based on the first impression.

Chapter 57

Chronological 'jump' to February 1869, twenty months on from the last action. Again there is factual documentation. There follows the girl watching the cab, her astonishment (this is a strongly visual but silent scene) which soon gives way to the aftermath. It is Mary who confides what she has seen (Sarah?) to Sam. More retrospect first, for Sam has ingratiated himself with Aunt Tranter, who provides the 'readies' until Sam ingratiates himself with Mr Freeman by the inspiration of his window-dressing. The upstairs/downstairs interaction which is a feature of the novel takes its ironic turn: Sam works for the man who could have been Charles's father-in-law.

Subjection of Women This important work echoes one of the main themes of this novel.
Girton College The Cambridge College for women founded in 1869 at Hitchin.
Catullus See note page 48.
en masse All together.
the last good crop ... Carslake's barn Wry cynical reference to the fact that Sam's and Mary's child was conceived there.
unchipper Sober, dull.
good wine needs no bush Proverbial expression – quality is its own recommendation.
The Faust myth ... The legend of selling your soul to the Devil – of doing wrong deliberately – derived from the wandering necromancer (c. 1488–1541), central character in Marlowe's *Dr Faustus* and Goethe's *Faust*.

Chapter 58

Charles travels all over the place, foresakes palaeontology, writes verse and carries Tennyson's *Maud* with him wherever he goes. The author chooses his own greatest poem of the period (Arnold's 'Yes: in the sea of life enisl'd') which was written (two years after Arnold's marriage) to Marguerite, whom he had met in 1848–9. The parallel with Charles will be apparent. Charles is bored, dreams, meets Americans, decides to go to America. It is quite obvious that Charles is escaping, travelling only until something definite happens, like the discovery of Sarah. Such is the narrative tension, that we sense that this cannot be far away.

sights, and sites Typically verbal sophistication – Fowles is supremely conscious of the sounds and effects of words.
khans and *alberghi* Inns.
Yes: in the sea of life enisl'd ... This beautiful and moving poem is central to Fowles' conception and themes – so important is it that we note the last line ends the final chapter of this story.

performed (or deformed) See note at the beginning of this chapter.
Canaan Genesis xii:5–10, the promised land.
speakables Words that can be spoken or expressed in speech.
Pocahontas (1595–1617) The daughter of an Indian chief, brought to
England after marrying a colonist.

Chapter 59

Documentation of the American (and particularly the Bos-
tonian) scene with particular reference to Henry James is under-
taken here. Charles gets on well, finds female society attractive,
but still thinks of the one face that could 'exorcise' his suffering.
Freeman's document weighs heavily on his actions. He sees too
in some of these faces 'a shadow of Sarah' (page 371). Careful
chronology follows Charles in a kind of wish-you-were-here tour
(it is December 1868), and his mixed reactions might be the
mixed reactions of an intelligent Englishman of our own time.
He finds it a successful escape, noting what he feels is the lack of
hypocrisy in America generally, and the atmosphere of 'anarchy'
in the South (just defeated in the American Civil War on the
issue of slavery). He writes a poem which salutes this new way of
life. Then, abruptly, he turns his back on it when he gets the
telegram announcing that Sarah has been found.

Bunker Hill i.e. the battle of Bunker's Hill near Boston, Massachusetts,
in the American War of Independence in which the English just
defeated the rebels (1775).
An even greater still The novelist Henry James (1843–1916): he
travelled extensively in Europe before settling in England in the town
of Rye. He became a naturalized Englishman in 1915.
the Lowell circle in Cambridge James Russell Lowell (1819–91)
American essayist and poet. Cambridge is in Massachusetts.
loxodromic Sailing obliquely (i.e. via Europe).
Civil War The American Civil War between the Northern and
Southern states on the question of slavery (1861–65).
ribbed about tea-parties i.e. the Boston tea-party of 1773, tipping tea
into the harbour in protest against the tea-tax which eventually led to
The American war of Independence.
sang-froid Composure, coolness.
farded Painted.
Andrew Johnson ... Ulysses S. Grant The first was President from
1865–69, the second from 1869–77.
carpet-baggers Northerners entering the Southern States after the
American Civil War and interfering in politics etc.

Albion's Britain's.

the iambic slog-and-smog and rhetorical question-marks An ironic comment on Charles's verses – the ten-beat rhythmic lines churned out with some obscurity and asking questions which aren't answered.

Chapter 60

It is now May (1869 presumably) when Charles is back in London. He goes to the house concerned, and the door is answered by a woman who is obviously far superior to a maid. The man who appears also seems to be free from convention. Charles realizes that he is in the house of an art collector who has lived through a scandal some twenty years earlier. He finds Sarah transformed, her dress manifestly that of the New Woman – colourful, independent, bohemian, perhaps a reflection of what she has become. At the same time all her distinctive qualities, of eyes, hair etc. are unchanged. There is the shock (supposedly) to her that Charles has broken his engagement to Ernestina. Charles's probing questions are unanswered: he realises he is in the house of a man of dangerous, unconventional reputation, and virtually assumes that Sarah is his mistress. The short sentences of Charles's thoughts reflect his anguish to know. Charles is here reacting conventionally to the situation, and Sarah proves that she has outstripped him in tolerance and enlightenment. She talks in analogies though – her natural ground has become art –but he misunderstands her (naturally) when she tells him there is someone else. She explains this superbly, and asserts her independence of marriage at the same time. Her fulfilment is her work, her pleasure at being in the company of genius, all this is finely conveyed: she asserts that although her companions have vices, these are not what the world imagines them to be. In a word, Sarah has developed, she has been given the opportunity to realize something of her potential. She has simply transcended her time. Charles sees clearly that she has achieved 'new self-knowledge and self-possession' (page 386). Charles intuitively sees too that she still suffers, and that she still lies. That is really the enigma that Sarah is. He believes that she hates him and, in him, all men. She won't accept this. It is obvious that there is a chemistry of rejection between them, with Charles feeling humiliated by what has happened. Sarah produces her trump card – her child, their child – but not before Charles has completely misinterpreted who he is about to see, thinking that it is the Rossetti's celebrated poetic sister, Christina. With Charles's fumbling for his watch we are reminded of the parallel situation of his temporary surrogate parenthood of the prostitute's child. The ensuing dialogue between Charles and Sarah is punctuated by Lalage. The upshot of it is that Sarah will not be possessed, that her 'parables' are not easily understood, that she is an enigma to the end. But even in this serious confrontation, the author finds the opportunity to be witty at the expense of the bad player of a Chopin mazurka who provides the background to the word and wordless exchanges between Charles and Sarah.

cachet Status.

the New Woman The feminist. But in 1868–9 they did not have the full backing of their sex, and one woman writer of some distinction, Eliza Lynn Linton, published anonymously a critical attack in her article 'The Girl of the Period' (1868).

amphora Greek or Roman two-handled vase.

soirée See note page 29.

'He shares this house with his brother' The reference is to the poet Dante Gabriel (1828–82) and to his brother the critic and man of letters William Michael Rossetti (1829–1919). Dante Gabriel's wife died in 1862; he buried his poems with her, and in the same year moved to Cheyne Walk, Chelsea.

John Morley (1838–1923) Editor of the *Fortnightly Review*, critic, man of letters, politician.

ménage à quatre – à cinq Household of four or five – with the implication of sexual looseness.

Mr Ruskin's John Ruskin (1819–1900) the great art critic and interpreter, also a great social idealist.

Noel Humphreys (1810–1879) Artist who published numerous works on natural history.

credo Expression of faith.

coup de grâce Finishing stroke.

like the poised-crumbling wall of a dam Note the vividly physical nature of the image.

Miss Christina Rossetti (1830–94) Sister of the two mentioned above. John Fowles obviously objects to her religiosity, but some of her poetry is very good indeed, arguably better than her brother's.

Language is like shot silk... A brilliant image to define verbal perspective.

a Chopin mazurka... Frederick Chopin (1810–49) the great Polish composer who lived in Paris from the age of twenty-one onwards.

his masts crashing... Another vivid image to express Charles's anguish.

Chapter 61

The important and mysterious personage (that is the right word), observer of most that has happened, takes his leave. We as mere readers return to the fictional scene. It is a variant on the one we have just witnessed between Sarah and Charles. Sarah appears to be offering Charles platonic friendship, but Charles feels that she has been manipulating him all the time. On the way out he meets the girl who had shown him up carrying a child. He knows that he must return to America and remain celibate. The author virtually explains the plausibility of this alternative ending, and Charles is left with the Arnold quotation as commentary on his forward way in life – 'And out again, upon the unplumb'd, salt, estranging sea.'

flânerie Dawdling, idling about.
Breguet French watch-maker of Swiss origin (1747–1823).
like the poised-crumbling walls of a dam The repetition of the phrase in order to capture deliberately the breaking of Charles's life.
soupirant Suitor, wooer.
A modern existentialist ... See note page 55 and consider the assertion which follows, and its link with the Arnold motto.
the unplumb'd, salt, estranging sea Arnold's line picked up here as separation, loneliness, the vast unknown.

Revision questions on Chapters 51–61

1 Write an essay on the reactions of Mary and Dr Grogan to Charles's treatment of Ernestina.

2 Again, through particular references to the text, indicate the role played by the author in these closing chapters.

3 In the confrontation scene with the lawyers, do you feel sorry for Charles or not? Give reasons for your answer.

4 Write an appreciation of the poem by Matthew Arnold quoted on pages 365–6. How is it related to the theme or themes of the novel?

5 Give an account of the last interviews between Charles and Sarah. Do you understand why each reacts as he/she does?

John Fowles's art in *The French Lieutenant's Woman*
Characterization

Every reader of *The French Lieutenant's Woman* must take note of the declared omniscience of the author. With most novels that we read we find there is a *straight* representation of character, by that I mean that however complex the person being described, he or she is an entity, a creation of slight or full aspects. With Fowles it is different in the sense that he tells you what his main characters do, and then changes it so that they do something else. The alternative ending, even to the extent of employing the same paragraphs with a different follow-up, shows you his emphasis on the fact that you are reading about characters in *fiction*: generally their lives are determined by him, sometimes he considers the alternatives before choosing one, and sometimes they take over themselves in a seeming independence of him. Not content with this, Fowles uses his voice in commentary or evaluation, as we have seen. Once or twice he even appears in the narrative himself – sitting opposite Charles in a railway carriage, or contemplating the Rossetti residence in Cheyne Walk. We presume this is him being close to his characters at critical junctures in their lives. But one effect of his reminders that they are *characters* is to inhibit our identification with them. For this, as readers, is what we tend to do – associate ourselves sympathetically (or the reverse) with the personalities we read about in fiction. I think we are with Jane in *Jane Eyre* when she is made to stand on the stool by the tyranny of Mr Brocklehurst: we are with Tess Durbeyfield when she strangles the dying birds after the shoot in *Tess of the D'Urbervilles*: and we are with Paul Morel in *Sons and Lovers* when he takes his mother out to tea in Nottingham. There is immediacy in *The French Lieutenant's Woman* and there is positive character creation too, but it is qualified by the author's reminding us of what we are doing.

The characters

Sarah Woodruff

she was born with a computer in her heart

Sarah is a figure of fascination, intriguing us the readers as much as she does Charles – and we can appreciate the strong physical and sympathetic draw she exerts over him. She is first seen in outline only, though dressed in the soul-destroying black which was the garb of the lower orders at the time. The black of course also signifies her mourning for the loss of her lover, but when she is described as being like 'a figure from myth' we immediately become aware that Sarah is to exist on the two levels – of reality on the one hand and of symbolic significance on the other.

I have chosen the quotation at the head of this study of her because she is intuitively an expert in deduction and appraisal. She greets Charles's first appeal to her (Chapter 2) without words but with a look charged with directness and insight. It pierces him like 'a lance' but it is significantly qualified by 'no artifice there, no hypocrisy, no hysteria, no mask ... no sign of madness'. Sarah's directness, which she keeps under control for the most part at Mrs Poulteney's, is one of her salient qualities.

John Fowles employs retrospect in order to integrate Sarah into the action in current time. This means taking us through Mrs Poulteney's motivations – where all *is* mask, hypocrisy, inverted hysteria and the madness of religiosity – and Sarah's story. But remember that it is a story at second-hand, told by the Vicar. To Mrs Poulteney she appears to be a sinner (an essential qualification). She is reserved and she is well educated (this might be regarded with suspicion). She cannot, even in her own interest, mask a certain independence, as when she refuses to discuss with Mrs Poulteney her continued feeling for the French Lieutenant. Pathos adheres to Sarah throughout, and most strongly at the end of her interview with Mrs Poulteney. She is able to look into the past and ponder the future over Lyme Bay; in practical terms, she has no money. Mrs Talbot's kind heart is moved by the fact that Sarah faces penury, and in an unobtrusive way – unobtrusive because it does not hold up the narrative – John Fowles is making a clear, unequivocal social and moral comment. Sarah's 'uncanny' ability to classify people (compare this with Darwin's classifications and, if you like, Charles's palaeontology). It is summed up in the phrase 'intellectual profundity of insight' and, together with her education, makes her unusual or, rather, remarkable, to use Charles's word. She cannot fit into her time – there is no niche for Sarah. Her lot in life is to inhabit the downstairs world whilst her intellect would more than qualify her for the upstairs life. In a word, she is a victim in a society which has rigid standards of class distinction.

Her history – her father's mental illness – is a conditioning factor but not as strong as those previously mentioned. Sarah soon displays the quality of her sympathy – in her saving of Millie in her trouble – a kind of natural Christianity in contradistinction to Mrs Poulteney's self-conscious religiosity. Sarah's insight is shown in the fact that she has 'twigged' Mrs Poulteney. Sarah's own religious feeling and her intense susceptibility are shown in her breaking down while she is reading. According to her creator, she sees through the narrowness and cant of the Victorian church, her prayers being for the relief of suffering and not in support of the observance of ritual. Her handling of the Tract Test shows her powers of self-control, her need to be solitary in the few walks she has reflects the grip her obsession has on her. She shows what is called her diplomacy by being present or not present according to the calibre and status of Mrs Poulteney's visitors. She also shows her sensitivity. Indeed, she is so self-contained in her fallenness that she inspires hatred – built on possessive jealousy – in Mrs Fairlie. Sarah goes along with Mrs Poulteney's request that she should not exhibit her shame. She smiles. She knows the inviolability of the heart.

Sarah is seen by Charles during his exploration of the Undercliff. It is a transfiguring moment, although he does not realize it then, and again we are aware of the enigmatic quality in Sarah, seen here in her silence – and silence is one of her characteristics, perhaps born of her situation. On the next occasion, when Charles is all apologies, she does speak, but it is to impress him to keep silent about meeting her. It also contains 'a most peculiar element of rebuffal'. Although she later succumbs, this reflects Sarah's self-containment. It is also seen when, Mrs Fairley having done her effective worst, Sarah is arraigned by Mrs Poulteney. She preserves her own dignity, but the effort it has cost her is seen at the close of the chapter. We are told that she is not looking out to sea for Satan's sails; she is crying silently as she stands on the edge of suicide.

It is at this stage that Fowles reminds the reader that he is writing fiction, and that the puppets are at his whim. They might have done this, we could have had a chapter on Sarah's state of mind ... instead we get a brief reference to the impact Charles has made on her. He makes an even greater impact the next time they meet when he helps her up on the steep path after she has slipped. In description the focus is on Sarah's eyes which, among other things, show her determination to be what she is in independence of convention. Charles sees this, but he also guesses that there may be 'darker qualities'. These may be in part obscure (I have said that Sarah is enigmatic) but the one that he fears to recognise is her sensuality.

In this exchange with Charles she reveals a degree of bitterness, but she also shows the quality of her obstinacy in saying that she will not leave Lyme. There is also a fatalistic finality about her which is seen in her *knowing* that Varguennes will never return. At their next meeting there is a further underlining of the impact Charles has made on her. She is anxious to confide in him, almost the release of her repressed needs, and Charles is struck anew by her unusual qualities. The overt gesture is to give him the *Micraster* tests, the real reason to thank him for offering her assistance and to talk. There is a terrible pathos about her admission that she has no one to turn to. What is even more moving is her recognition that if she goes to London she will be forced onto the streets – she will in fact become the scarlet woman that she is locally credited with being. She also fears her capacity to sin – she is undergoing a penance in Lyme – but it is keeping her out of trouble. Her outpouring is an indictment of Christian hypocrisy, the revelation of how acutely she is suffering her fate. It is the prelude to her confession. That is delayed, and Charles has his conversation with and part-confession to Grogan. The break in the chapter leads us deliberately back to Sarah and her innocent, protective affection for Millie which gives them the physical comfort of each other's nearness. Sarah is meek to Charles, tells the story directly and simply – and lies, as we discover later. This is one of the reasons why I say that she is an enigma – it is almost as if she wishes to martyr herself. The state of nervous tension she is in as she tells the details is very interesting; she defoliates 'the milkwort' and underlines the fact that her life has been so lonely. She also shows some social awareness of the sufferings of others. When she says that she gave herself to Varguennes she qualifies her own motives, seeing herself as typifying the suffering 'in every town and village in this land'. It is a moving but perhaps rather too self-conscious association, almost as if she has taken on the radical voice of her author. Paradoxically, she feels that in being 'the French Lieutenant's Whore' she has achieved a kind of freedom. The question immediately arises as to whether Sarah really knows herself. Charles, following his conversation with Grogan, naturally feels that he is in the presence of madness, so intent is Sarah on playing the role of self-styled outcast. Such is her presence however (and a vague hint of suicide too) that Charles is compelled by her. Yet in what she says there is a strange clear-headedness – solitude hurts no one, but walking your shame down a main street means that you are condemned. Generously, she interprets his interest as kindness, only asking for time to reflect. When she leaves she sends Charles the note which at once puts him into Sam's hands and starts their own urgent love affair – though neither of them are aware of that yet.

Before that we have another retrospect – this time covering Sarah's confrontation with Mrs Poulteney. It is brief but telling, Sarah having the courage of her experience to indict Mrs Poulteney for hypocrisy and being brave enough to suggest that she buys an instrument of torture, since this is what she is best at. Afterwards we find her broken down in prayer, probably for the sin she has just committed. How glad we are that she did. The cut to the barn in the next chapter (31) is cinematic in its speed and dramatic effect. Although she feels herself in error – she apologizes to Charles for having caused him so much trouble – she is also impetuous and impassioned, as she shows when she seizes his hand and raises it towards her lips. In a word, she is 'all flame'. We are aware of her strong, sensually direct nature, and Charles is aware of it to the point of embarrassment. Her intention cannot be mistaken. Charles is overcome, yet at the moment of their kissing he feels her fragility, her vulnerability. He also senses her wildness. She acknowledges her own remarkable

nature, but she does it with a bitter simplicity. In effect she has
shown her love for Charles to him, and reaped the response of
his convention. She becomes obedient (she is inwardly frus-
trated) and agrees to go to Exter. At this moment she is way
ahead of Charles in emotional capacity. But he does not want to
read that language.

Exeter reveals a different Sarah, a woman who for the first
time in her life is able to buy – and delight in – the small
purchases which give her some small compensation, a sense of
identity. The nightgown and the bandage both suggest, I feel,
that just as she has waited for Varguennes, so now she waits for
Charles. Fowles reminds us that she belongs to her time, and her
eating the meat pie without delicacy is a touch of ironic realism.
Charles's appraisal of her that she is 'shrewd and sensitive'
strikes us as being an accurate one.

The accident which traps Sarah in the hotel room awaiting
Charles is a lie, like her lie about having given herself to
Varguennes. She wants Charles to come, she wants to give herself to him, and she wants to be physically trapped, not to bind
Charles to her (though that is possible) but to enjoy him and
have him enjoy her. There is a certain masochism in Sarah – but
the joy will be more than the hurt. Their sexual coming together
is passionate but it is also brutal, demanding, hurting. Charles
has at last broken his own resistance: Sarah had already broken
hers.

Sarah's 'remarkable' nature is shown in her attitude after the
love-making. She makes no demands, stresses the social differences between them, and then comes the revelation of her
virginity, and the fact that 'There was no strained ankle'. Fowles
is quick to give the reactions of the male mind – Charles suspects
blackmail, the motive being to trap him – but Sarah has a simple
dignity and at this moment a transcendent sincerity. She forces
him to leave, apparently content with the experience of this day.
It may be, however, that with her 'computer' she accurately
gauges this man *and* her own nature. More pertinently, she
knows too the social, moral and legal mores of her time. We are
told that she is calm and fatalistic: she tells Charles bluntly that
he could have no happiness with her. We feel that she is
speaking a deep truth.

Sarah disappears from the action for a long period. She is
seen in London by Mary in February 1869: on the last day of

May Charles comes to her in Cheyne Walk where she is living under the protection of the Rossettis. His first sight of her sufficiently indicates her development – I nearly said 'change', but I think development the right word because of her remarkable qualities and the independence of her spirit. She is the New Woman – freed from convention, able to develop her mind and her emotions. She has come a long way from the teapot and the meat pie of Endicott's Hotel. Charles recognises the essential Sarah beneath all this, but it does him little good. His questions – and his self-interest – only serve to show that her integrity is greater than his imagination. She has come to an intellectual equality with him, and he recognises that her directness of language is the major part of her individuality. Sarah's sensitivity, the whole mobility of her development, is seen in her defining for Charles the kind of life she leads and the rewards she gains from it. She has had the independence to overcome convention, and although she feels for Charles she asks for his understanding of her position and the fulfilment it has brought her. Charles however does see into the enigma, and the quotation must be given in full if we are to appreciate and apprehend Sarah:

And perhaps he did at last begin to grasp her mystery . . . it was not that she hated man, not that she materially despised him more than other men, but that her manoeuvres were simply a part of her armoury, mere instruments to a greater end. He saw deeper still; that her supposed present happiness was another lie. In her central being she suffered still, in the same old way; and that was the mystery she was truly and finally afraid he might discover. (Chapter 60).

But Sarah's final bluff is called: she reveals the existence of their child so that Charles may not misunderstand her. She knows, with that truth to herself that is her distinguishing quality, that what she has said to Charles had to be said, that he will never understand her. Or does she do all this? Or is the child in the 'alternative ending' theirs? The enigma of the ending is in fact the enigma of Sarah. The remarkable, completely distinctive heroine, who has eluded us for so long, eludes us – and Charles – at the end. She is, as Fowles makes ironically clear, a character in fiction and her reality depends on his whim.

Charles

And he had always asked life too many questions

Charles has his scientific interests, his inheritance (until part of it, though not a really substantial part, is removed from him by his uncle's remarriage) is more than adequate, he has status, intellect, culture, a good sense of humour. His wealth makes him able to indulge his interest in palaeontology: he has a genuine interest in nature, and this puts him apart from his contemporaries who are largely of the hunting, shooting kind (consider the different attitudes of Charles and his uncle over the shooting of the Great Bustard). Charles's doubts – the characteristic doubts of the period – find him rejecting the Church (he is sent to Paris to counteract *that* temptation) and becoming an agnostic. He is also non-political, though a secret admirer of the Liberal Gladstone. He is eminently marriageable, though to many of the mamas and their pretty daughters who try to trap him he appears cold and aloof. In other words, Charles is ripe for experience in life since he obviously finds the superficiality of society tame. And that is largely what *The French Lieutenant's Woman* is about. His first meeting with the silent Sarah on the Cobb (he calls her ironically 'My good woman') is heavy with the unknown, the mystical, the compelling. Charles does not yet understand this. Charles is a frank egoist who is seen ironically by his author: there are a number of telling moments of self-exposure when Charles countemplates himself, notably after his first exchange with Sam, whom he has accused of being fast (tongue in cheek of course). He enjoys the role of tolerant young master he has set himself to play. Looking at himself prior to covering his face with lather, he decides that he has breeding and self-knowledge: both are to be put to the test in the course of his encounters with Sarah and his relationship with Ernestina.

Charles in fact enjoys his premarital freedom, for Ernestina is subject to moods and migraines. His being equipped for his expeditions is treated with visual irony, but the effect is to make Charles just a little ridiculous. Yet it makes us respond to him too. His interest amounts to a kind of dedication, but always we are aware of the fact that he has the means and the leisure to indulge it. Outside this, until he meets Sarah – and Sarah the prostitute – he has little knowledge of life itself despite the fact that he has gone through a gentleman's statutory initiation of paid-for sex. At this stage we form the impression that he is, if anything, undersexed or, perhaps more accurately, that the society in which he lives has undersexed him.

On 29 March 1867 Charles explores the Undercliff and unknowingly explores his inner self when he meets Sarah. His impressionability is shown immediately he looks down on the sleeping Sarah and his sexual response – immediate but not articulated – is clear too. His breeding pretty soon kills off any natural interchange, though at this stage Sarah herself would not have welcomed it. He walks away not, his author assures us, down the wrong path: but the impression of incomprehension and the influence of Sarah's eyes remain with him. They are an insidious compulsion, at first not honestly met, towards further meetings. And at this stage John Fowles gives us the necessary retrospect on Charles and how he came to be engaged to Ernestina. In fact the latter had made him aware that life was passing him by. As always he is torn between two courses at the moment of crisis. He thinks that he will travel: but hardly has he said this than he takes the other path – he becomes engaged to Ernestina. This retrospect is broken into by the urgency of the present. Charles is inquisitive about Sarah, and questions the dairyman. When he hears her called the 'French Loot'n'nt's Hoer' he is appalled. Charles has a chivalrous, kindly streak, and he employs it to apologise to Sarah. He is conscious – in some ways Charles is enlightened – that she is victim, that she is being treated barbarously.

Just as John Fowles gives Sarah alternative actions and teases the reader at the same time, so he takes the reader into his confidence (winking at the same time) about Charles – about what he would have him do and what he does. He is confessing, in fact, what George Eliot once observed: that a character in fiction is almost capable of becoming independent of its author, who is forced to acknowledge that independence. Charles's next interaction with Sarah is in the presence of Mrs Poulteney, Ernestina and Mrs Tranter, and her reactions absorb his attention. He is perceptive enough to see that Sarah's meekness constitutes determined repression, and that she is suffering from a sense of injustice. Charles is not just superficial in society, and manages to be sarcastic to Mrs Poulteney, an action which calls forth the reader's approval. More than that, it calls forth an identification with Sarah – she and Charles know Mrs Poulteney for what she is.

Charles continues to tease Sam, without realizing that Sam's interest in Mary is a downstairs equivalent to his own passion, as yet unrealized, for Sarah. He participates in the indolence of life in Ernestina's company, hearing her read aloud but bored out of his mind, despite his occasional wit. But he is of course living for the next meeting with Sarah. When it comes he behaves again with chivalry and kindness. He sees Sarah's unusualness but, typically, equates it with a different class of woman. He is enlightened enough however to adjust his stance and not be prejudiced against her. He intends to do good to her, approaching the subject through the kindness and concern for her he has observed in Mrs Tranter. As yet he is not really involved or, as the author puts it, he is 'smiling, at ease in all his travel, his reading, his knowledge of a larger world'. It is this kind of comment which assures us of the author's ironic tone.

But now we come to Charles's real motivation, and again I suggest that he does not recognise it. He urges Sarah to leave the district. On the face of it this is sound anyway, but we suspect that he is actuated by *fear*, fear of his own involvement with her. He even has the insensitivity to raise the question of Sarah's sanity with her, although not necessarily subscribing to belief in it. This, I think, is a way of persuasion that is tantamount to emotional blackmail. At the back of all this is his knowledge of Ernestina and genuine attempt to continue his relationship with her. Already the undermining process here has begun, for he is becoming irritated with her and conscious of the superficiality which aids and abets charm and monotony. And Charles is very afraid of being bored. He knows too about her jealousy, and this conditions his silence about Sarah. He feels that perhaps he has been precipitate with regard to marriage – one of his reasons for travelling so much has been his objections to the conventionality, and now in all the Englishness of his nature he has willingly embraced it.

The presentation of Charles runs the length of the book, and I do not wish to extend the discussion too much here. By concentrating on a few incidents one can see into the heart of Charles, a heart which he succeeds in concealing from himself for a long time. Sarah's great inroad into his emotions is that 'She made him aware of a deprivation'. That deprivation is called life.

He deliberately courts trouble, or at least commitment, by returning to Sarah's haunts. He realizes that she is becoming interested in him. He is touched by the present of the sea-urchins. But still he holds fast to convention and the impropriety of being seen with her. At this stage we feel that Charles is dishonest, a moral coward. He finds that Sarah's independence – she even dares to contradict him – is part of her fascination, but he feels too that he must escape from the predicament he finds himself in. His ungenerosity is such that he feels that scandal will embrace him, or even that Sarah will blackmail him (this comes to him later after the moment of their consummation). Yet he still agrees to meet her again in order to hear her confession. He knows it is madness (he chooses the more polite word 'folly') and he consults Dr Grogan, though his approach to this *is* devious and dishonest. The encounter shakes Charles to his sexual core. When she has told her story (the most important part of it a lie) Charles wishes that he could have enjoyed her as Varguennes supposedly did. He forgives Sarah what she says she has done, and although he cannot completely free himself from his prejudices, he has been won to her the more deeply by her account. Full of Grogan's theories, he still urges upon her the need to move away. It is becoming increasingly apparent that it is his need (in his own mind) that she should do so. When Sam and Mary nearly, accidentally, discover them, Sarah smiles, and this sparks off in Charles a strongly passionate sexual response. He nearly succumbs.

Afterwards Charles feels an overwhelming and selfish relief. He also faces the immediate prospect of Winsyatt. He rides this news very well, but his heart misses a beat when he hears that Sarah has been dismissed by Mrs Poulteney. He too entertains the feeling, since she is missing, that there may be real cause for alarm. He is both relieved and irritated by another note from Sarah, then erupts into jealousy. What he does not realize now is that he has given himself away to Sam by the sheer irrationality of his behaviour. Sam, the sharp domestic, has brought Charles a supper-tray, but is forcefully told to eat the meal himself.

In the post-Winsyatt experience Charles becomes more than ever dissatisfied with Ernestina. He has the self-realization to confess to Grogan, and the terms he uses to explain the fascination are, I think, appropriate: 'I feel like a man possessed against his will.' He is desperate to be rid of Sarah, and now entertains Grogan's idea that she ought to be in an asylum. But he keeps to the appointment. When he sees her sleeping he feels protective, sexually moved but cannot explain his feelings to himself. He is being asked to forgive, but he cannot give himself. When he takes her into his arms – and he feels her slightness and vulnerability – he cannot do anything but resist his deeper nature. The result is that he pushes her away. And then, to compound chaos, Sam and Mary see them.

Charles is always concerned for his reputation – or perhaps one should say the preservation of his respectable image. Having got rid of Sam and Mary he insults Sarah in the guise of generosity – he gives her money, blames himself for 'engaging her affections' (what a woefully inadequate phrase), tells her that there is talk in the town of 'committing you to an institution' and then suggests that she walk part of the way back so that there will be no scandal for him. This supreme selfishness – this fear of commitment, a denial of his feelings and inner identity – shows just how unequal to Sarah (at this stage) Charles is. He even shakes hands with her at parting: he raises his hat to her when he sees her standing where he left her. Charles is still ruled by propriety.

He decides to go to London – a natural reflex action, though of course it means leaving Ernestina behind. Charles is unequal, we suspect, to coping with her. But before he sets out he takes good care to bribe Mary to silence. He sees Ernestina's father, and is somewhat humiliated by what happens. Charles is a natural Victorian snob, and regards any participation in 'trade' with horror. He is also undermined by seeing a nursemaid lovingly greet a soldier, and this makes him aware of his 'deprivation'. Charles is adept at resisting the pressures put on him by Mr Freeman, but his pleas of ignorance do not get him very far. Nevertheless he feels the more acutely after this the futility of his own existence.

Charles is now ripe for debauch – the attempt to forget yourself in sensual 'enjoyment' – and is easily persuaded by his club companions (impeccable in their social credentials) to join them. Although Fowles tells us that Charles is not merely a snob and that he is overcoming history, he also tells us that he does not know it. He has got to be very sick first.

At Ma Terpsichore's he is disgusted and irritated, but this is motivation to escape. He finds the other Sarah, and although the atmosphere of their encounter is not entirely convincing – she is too much the tart with the heart – it nevertheless indicates certain facets of Charles's character which are important. Firstly, despite his suffering he is considerate and, when it comes to both this Sarah and her child, kind. Not only is he practical and generous in giving the extra money, he is also concerned, asking questions, probing socially and morally: he is also appreciative of the practical sympathy he gets. Another interesting aspect of this experience is that it puts him directly into the orbit of life as distinct from the void he fears.

All he gets is Sarah's address and Sam's ambitions for himself, a lightly cloaked form of blackmail, for Sam can tell which way things are going. Charles is still resistant, and his reaction to the fact that there is no begging letter or confession of guilt is to return to Ernestina. There he takes up the reins of courtship, or so we are led to believe. But we have been conned. That is what the better part of him wished to do, but in fact he went to Exeter and straight to Endicott's Hotel. Sam, that potential, although soon to be practical blackmailer is in attendance. But Charles goes to Sarah's arms, and takes a virgin. This is enough to make him moral, suspicious, and Sarah sees through him and into him. The result is that she calls him Mr Smithson, but his life is irrevocably changed.

Charles then goes to the church, and the change is deepened not only by his self-questioning and prayer but by the depth of his feelings – by his emotional as well as his rational self. He undergoes strong Christ associations, and suddenly, in a moment of illumination, sees the meaning of love, life, and the real religion of Christianity – 'To uncrucify'. In a word he rejects death and the past, and lives for the future. Sarah has won.

He writes to her, telling her what he intends to do. Hitherto ruled by convention and fear of discovery – fear too of self-discovery, one suspects – he takes his journey to Lyme. He even takes in the possibilities of Sam, but this does not deflect him. His scene with Ernestina shows how hard and resilient he can be. In the course of it he lies, but he gains his own identity. He now knows that the world he has lived in has made him an impostor. The real world with Sarah, he believes, awaits him. He rides out the condemnation of Grogan and the notice of Sam, his initial rage calmed by the thought of seeing Sarah. He is somewhat comforted too by Grogan's retraction and his wishing him well. But Sarah's non-appearance is to set him off on that travelling trail which he has threatened to embrace earlier. Before he does so he prays that he will find Sarah. This simple act endears us to him: he is frail, in need of help and love. Science is no protection against vulnerability. In a superb chapter (55) Charles meets, without knowing, his creator. I say 'meets' in the fictional sense of the term, for the author indicates that he doesn't know what to do with him. He decides to have him pass on through the suffering and the humiliation, the first emotional, the second legal.

There follows the return from abroad, the poetry which precedes it giving us an insight into the man, whose talents are not great in terms of this kind of composition. Arnold, as the author indicates, has put it better and with a kind of terrifying finality. Charles's taste of America, his small ritual dissipations, all contribute to his occupying himself until the message of hope arrives. Faced with the New Woman Charles is forced to lose sight of the old. He is shocked but in some ways relieved, for Sarah has not become a prostitute like her namesake. She even looks younger. Charles is bewildered too, rather overcome, by the Bohemian association with the Rossettis, and the fear that she is the mistress of Dante Gabriel. All his expectations are defeated, for he had really thought that he would find her in poverty and need and that he would elevate her. In fact, Sarah is elevated by her experiences, Charles weighed down by what he sees and the bourgeois nature of his suspicions. Although he has been brave in making the break earlier, he has not conquered his Victorian inheritance. She is his intellectual equal, and Victorian man was hardly ready for that. Charles is generous enough to offer Sarah the continuance of what she has now, but his mind is small enough to entertain jealousy of what he believes is her preference for another. The 'alternative ending' now bulks large, and Charles tries to comfort Lalage (as he comforted the other Sarah's baby) *or* he refuses Platonic friendship, and walks away. He is a 'character' in a fiction, and his author cunningly describes two might-have-beens to round off his appearances in these pages. Suffice to say that we often feel for Charles and with Charles, but that whereas his reactions are recognizable and predictable Sarah's aren't – and Sarah's are too much for him. Tied to his time, he transcends it by one gesture of revolt which changes the course of his (fictional) existence. He cannot however escape the enigma (the Sphinx of the last paragraph) who has compelled him despite all the odds of downstairs/upstairs blackmail. Charles can have no real conception of what Sarah has achieved by her position in the Rossetti household. This is his limitation.

Other characters

Ernestina

Ernestina is given a greater degree of life and individuality than one might expect. At first one is inclined to attribute to her a kind of superficiality, but this is unfair. She is clearly a product of her time, dresses in the height of fashion, has a natural fund of society small talk, and is very aware of the difference in her social caste and Charles's. She is somewhat in awe of her father, the self-made man who has set his face against the progress inherent in the conclusions of Darwin. There is a teasing streak in her nature which is quite endearing, but hers is a largely indolent life, a compound of headaches and journal writing, of pondering and becoming moody, though her spirit is more positive than might appear initially. She can lower her eyes prettily and becomingly, but she can also hint that there is a little bit of the bitchiness of Becky Sharp in her make-up. She has been spoilt and cossetted, has the usual sexual hang-ups of the time, just occasionally peering beneath the surface to think of the possibility of passion, but she is ignorant and frightened about sex.

And that is not the only thing that makes for fear. She is uncertain of Charles – he is eleven years older than she is – knows that he has had experiences in, for instance, Paris and Lisbon, and feels that he may be 'flirting' with other women when she is not there. She is of a naturally jealous disposition (witness her treatment of Mary). Here she demonstrates the natural Victorian reflex of upstairs snobbery – Mary is only a servant. Fowles says of Ernestina, however, that she is not 'a domestic tyrant but simply a horrid spoilt child'. In capturing Charles she has displayed a certain low cunning: she never flings herself at him, engages his heart, and cries becomingly when he proposes to her.

Ernestina is senstive. She blames herself when Charles is snubbed by Mrs Poulteney. But when she reads Mrs Norton's poem to Charles she shows that she has a sense of humour – the 'mutton-bone' rhyme sufficiently reprimanding his inattention. Her nose is put out of joint by the loss of Winsyatt and the consequent loss of status, though she says that she feels it on Charles's account. She reveals herself to Charles in a way which he can only describe to himself as 'unladylike', though she is quick to realise the role that she must play in order to soothe him. After this we feel some accretion of pity for Ernestina. She is virtually removed from the action until Charles's crisis of confession and rejection. The spoilt child has no inkling of what is going on. She faces the biggest shock of her life with passion, with vehemence, with the spirit we have suspected lurking within her. Before this she confides to her diary her own lack of breeding, linking it to a cloying prayer. She takes great care in her preparations to greet Charles, but his intention of going to London brings out her wilful and sullen side.

When Charles tells her of his decision Ernestina reacts with 'bitter primness', but there is a surprising maturity in her telling Charles, when she is given the chance to speak at length, that she had hoped to give him faith in himself. It is unusual, unexpected, and shows that there is more depth to Ernestina than we had thought. She sees that Charles is lying, she feels her intense shame, and she determines on the legal recourse to revenge. When she faints we know she is acting. It is her last resource, but she has shown temper, passion and individual strength before this occurs.

Mrs Poulteney

Mrs Poulteney is a dragon of religiosity. Given the novelist's licence to create 'characters', Fowles has drawn for us a fearful, hypocritical, larger-than-life grotesque. We cannot help feeling that the radical Fowles rejects and pillories what she represents, and what she represents in inquisitorial Christianity of the worst and most despicable kind. She is repressive, mean, tyrannical, thinking to buy herself a place in heaven by the rigour of her despotism and the denial of freedom to those she employs. Employs is perhaps the wrong word: humiliates and degrades would be more accurate. By taking a sinner like Sarah into her house she feels she is promoting an act of carefully calculated charity. She is in fact merely exercising power, the sadism of torture. The fact that all that she does is in the name of Christianity only makes it worse. Sex has been driven deeply underground: it will never surface above the mantraps. She reduces all that she touches: she cannot be contradicted. In a brilliant fantasy Fowles has her approaching Heaven, she is rejected, and consigned to Hell. Sarah sees into her and through her. She puts her down with a rare, outspoken brevity. But afterwards she prays, perhaps for forgiveness of her sins, but also for the woman whose reginal presence (maybe a parody of Queen Victoria) is a lasting indictment of the repressive anti-Christian nature of so much expressed Christianity.

Dr Grogan

Dr Grogan is a grotesque too, but an endearing one in some ways. His discussion with Charles is one of the high points of the novel in terms of scientific appraisal laced with a degree of wit. But he is also biased, caught up in his theories of madness. What is likeable about him is that although he feels protective about the rejection of Ernestina he is big enough to forgive Charles and wish him well. Perhaps it would be true to say – and I feel that it fits the character anyway – that although he growls a lot he doesn't bite. There is a native canniness about him, he is shrewd and can be pungent.

Mrs Tranter

Mrs Tranter only comes alive fitfully, but she is good-hearted and anxious to keep the peace. She is harmless and does not interfere, though she is certainly upset on Ernestina's account when Charles breaks the engagement.

For the most part the rest are caricatures – Charles's uncle, Mr Freeman, even the prostitute Sarah, who is, I suppose, a good influence on Charles through the association of her child.

Sam and Mary

Two characters remain to be considered in some detail, and these are of course *Sam* and *Mary*. Both are, I would submit, recognisably caricature, and Fowles is not at his happiest in reproducing the cockneyisms of Sam and the local dialect of Mary. That they are intended as caricature there is no doubt – the upstairs/downstairs interaction is central to the novel – and their function is important. Sam, as his creator freely acknowledges, owes much to Dickens's brilliant evocation of Sam Weller – Mr Pickwick's servant whose wit and humour is a continual refreshment to the reader. He pronounces on life: this Sam, servant to an unPickwickian character, is fast, sharp, intent on number one. His response to Mary and the bag of soot, followed by his determined courtship of her, shows him in typical action. He is persuasive, having at the back of his mind the idea that Charles as employer and patron will help to set him up in a shop. Mary's ambition does not look beyond this, though she has a natural feminine interest in dress and goes along with Sam's schemes. Sam's ambition (ironically Charles had been the first to recommend him) is more than furthered by Mr Freeman, who is not dissimilar to Sam in outlook, given their different social strata. Both are in trade: their object is to make money. Mary, on the other hand, though she is pretty, pert and forward, is obviously intended to slot into domesticity in the usual Victorian fashion. This she does, but she also has a functional role. In supporting Sam in his ambitions she automatically comforts her mistress in her distress, her eye on the main chance here too. She also has the function of spotting Sarah, the news then being conveyed via the agent to Charles. I am not suggesting here that Sam and Mary are merely gold-diggers, they are more than that. They are a young couple making their way in life and, in view of their social positions, they have to take, and make, anything they can get. Both have endearing qualities and both are born sur-vivors.

Style

This single word cannot do justice to the vivacity and verve of John Fowles's style. He is the master of the various modes which make for stimulating and vivid writing.

In the screenplay, Harold Pinter had the good sense and artistic awareness to retain much of Fowles's original *dialogue*. Take the first exchange between Ernestina and Charles about 'poor Tragedy', It has the immediate ring of truth – it sounds right in any period. Take too the exchanges between Charles and Sarah, both in their ramblings or, indeed, in the passionate coming together in Chapter 46 and their conversation in the following chapter. Fowles's main achievement in the use of dialogue is the variety he is able to employ. Consider, for example, the differences in tone and mood which are conveyed by the following: Charles's conversation with the prostitute both before and after he is sick. Compare this immediately with the 'club' conversation which Charles has before he and his temporary friends set off for Ma Terpsichore's. Here you have a contrasting social range, and this is given greater extension if you look at any two conversations between Charles and Sam on the one hand, or any conversation between Sam and Mary, including the one where they are established in domesticity and reasonable prosperity. In fact there are high watermarks of conversational exchange and interaction in the novel, none better, I would suggest, than the final one (first version) between Charles and Sarah. A further examination would, I think, yield up the quality shown in Charles's rejection of Ernestina (look particularly at her words), in Mrs Poulteney's interrogation of the Vicar about Sarah (and then her interrogation of Sarah), and finally, the dramatic legal discussion in which Charles is humiliated. Although the teasing about character runs throughout, the fact is that Fowles creates convincing characters through their speech and in one or two cases, convincing caricatures through their speech.

If dialogue provides fiction with the drama of situation in which character finds itself, then I think it true to say that *description* is the natural adhesive of narration. The initial description of Lyme, of the Cobb, the Undercliff, the background overlooking the bay which becomes the foreground of Charles's scientific discoveries and love-enlarging encounters, all is done with a kind of loving association. Interiors too, whether at Mrs Poulteney's, or in London, or at Winsyatt (this too is a fine exterior) are finely done. Always with Fowles you are given a sense of actuality, and this is enhanced by a discreet but telling use of *metaphor* and *simile*. These are sometimes sudden, often brief, often rich. They are the jewels in the crown of Fowles's style (see the textual notes which pick out some, or search for your own as Charles searches the Undercliff). They glitter with the quality of his imagination. Fowles's language is resonant and vital. There are no boring or bathetic periods. The writing is vigorous with life.

The *irony* runs throughout – in fact the whole conception of the novel set in 1867–69 but written with the hindsight of what has happened since then is ironic through perspective and convention. Sarah perhaps is not seen ironically, but Charles certainly is – a dabbling scientist who ducks reality and observes convention despite his own scepticism. The upstairs/downstairs interaction is an ironic appraisal of social caste and motive. Occasionally the irony bursts into a more outspoken area – the *satire* which embraces (with a kind of barbed wire) the reginal hypocrisy, the tyrannical religiosity, of Mrs Poulteney. But for the most part irony plays over situation, social nuance, character in action: or its light is cast on moral and sexual mores, like the visit to Ma Terpsichore's or even Charles's visit to Winsyatt. The fact that the observer is detached is itself ironic. As he puts it in the preface to the screenplay 'I know I am, like most novelists, far too corrupted by and addicted to the solitary freedoms of prose fiction (where the one megalomaniac plays producer, director, all the cast *and* camera).' *The authorial voice* is also a distinguishing mark of Fowles's style. Its Victorian antecedents have already been mentioned, but Fowles's voice is loaded with contemporary references (by contemporary I mean Victorian), conveying the flavour of historical authenticity throughout. That voice evidences his own research, the documents of the period on which the fiction is reared. In addition – what he has called the 'stereoscopic vision' – is important. This is the modern perspective, the twentieth-century consciousness, the seemingly casual references, for example, to Nazism, the inclusion of an epigraph from William Manchester's *The Death of President Kennedy*, and the reference to discoveries which shed light on the Victorian period. Darwin is a case in point, seen from now as well as from then. Add to this Grogan's comments on the nature of madness, the particular case cited from the past but evaluated from the twentieth-century present, and you have the Fowlesian method in *The French Lieutenant's Woman*. His learning is sometimes casual, and we get the impression of someone who has saturated himself in the period, reproducing both what he researched in depth and what he remembers as details.

Although Pinter further economized Fowles's conception (and added two characters of his own) the fact is that Fowles is a generally economical writer. Where he is not so it appears that he is either subscribing to and even parodying the Victorian conception of length with plenty of authorial guidance. Thus there are two or three chapters which are devoted to authorial commentary – practically one, for example, on Hardy and his (supposed) relationship with his cousin Tryphena Sparks. Many of the comments are related to sociological findings about the period, some to the political background, many of course on the situation of women, symbolized in the particular case of Sarah. Fact is often present in the fiction, cunningly mixed, as in the Rossetti household in Chapter 60. Arguably the authorial weighting holds up the narrative, but it also has a quality of supportive authenticity about it. Having determined to write a certain kind of novel Fowles does it, so to speak, with a fullness of texture enclosing his text – the main storyline about Sarah and Charles.

I have been deliberately brief in this section, which is linked to both the *Structure* and the *Settings* of the novel, since Fowles has a wonderful sense of what the best Victorian novelists had – total relevance, to use Henry James's phrase here. Style is often commented on in the textual notes, but *Structure* is the shape or form of the novel as a whole.

Structure

Because of the ambiguities and alternatives that the author suggests, the structure of *The French Lieutenant's Woman* has an unusual flexibility. For example, does Charles get off at Lyme or Exeter on his return from London? Well . . . Fowles gives us one, then the other. The result is a plastic art, aesthetically pleasing to the reader once that reader responds to the *spirit* of what he has before him. Characters develop, the author develops them, or they even develop themselves (perhaps). Because of this the formal framework of the novel – straight beginning, middle, unambiguous end – must be bent to accommodate Fowles's new conception. The structure of *The French Lieutenant's Woman* is therefore a combination of the narrative – the story line – and the narrator/author – treatment and comment on the characters he is making fit that story line. There is of course, as other sections of this commentary will indicate, much more to it than that. But this is the basic structure and it is, in terms of treatment, virtually unique in English fiction. One would have to go back to the eighteenth-century English novelist Laurence Sterne (1713–68) for any comparable treatment.

Settings

These are, I think, brilliantly conceived. It is worth looking closely at the first chapter of the novel, and then looking on to the meetings between Charles and Sarah, to get the full flavour of Lyme and its environs. I have said elsewhere that the descriptions are done with loving association, but that association deepens into felt, experienced, known detail. Here Fowles is superbly the novelist of place, but it would be unwise just to focus on Lyme. The London settings of club and prostitute's room are convincing, and even better, however repugnant it may be to some readers, is the evocation of that pornographic grotesque, Ma Terpsichore's. In a sense this is a timeless setting, one that will occur in every age because of the needs of the flesh. But here it is given a striking authenticity, not just because of the interior (copulative representational details) but because of the description of West End London at licentious leisure which precedes it. Nor should we forget Fowles's evocation of Exeter in absorbing detail, his capturing of the expanse and the particularity of Winsyatt, or the final sequences in the Rossetti house in Cheyne Walk. The American scenes are less vividly presented, but the sense of travel, of space, of movement, is somehow equated with the expansive development of the two leading characters. We begin in Lyme and we end in London: there is a wealth of difference between the two, just as there is now a wealth of difference between the two characters who have made their separate journeys. I suppose that settings and structure are closely related too, for Sam and Mary have come a similar journey but with a difference. Basically, Fowles is superbly the creator of the spirit of place.

General questions

1 Write an essay on the character of Sarah and what she represents in the novel.

Suggested notes for essay answer:
Remember throughout that Sarah is a created 'character' – insofar as you can judge she represents the following – the New Woman (by the end) – victim – status of women in society – moral attitudes towards 'fallen' women – possibility for woman who tries to be independent – development of maturity – culture – freedom from convention despite its pressures. These largely belong to the second part of the question. The first part might consider: her need for isolation – her love/hatred with the role she assumes – her need to repress herself (Mrs Poulteney) – her saving of Minnie (and affection for her) – her strongly individual nature – lies (why) – sensuality – intelligence – pleasure in simple things – growing love for Charles – reaction after their lovemaking – 'remarkable' nature – final sequence at the Rossettis.

2 Write an essay on the author's use of his own voice in the novel, saying what effect the various aspects of it have on you as a reader.
3 Give an account of any two scenes in the novel which you find *either* sad *or* humorous.
4 What do you feel about Charles? Do you feel sorry for him, impatient with him, or what? Refer to the text in support of what you say.
5 Write an essay on the author's use of irony or satire in the novel or both.
6 In what ways do you think John Fowles is critical of the period about which he is writing? Refer to the text in support of what you say.
7 Write an account of any two situations in the novel which are set away from the main location of Lyme. What do they contribute to the story?
8 Indicate the part played in the plot by Sam and Mary. Do you find their roles convincing?
9 Write on the way the author's twentieth-century viewpoint

makes its presence felt in the narrative of *The French Lieutenant's Woman*.

10 Write an appreciation of the author's descriptive powers *or* of his use of figurative language in the novel.

11 Write character sketches of Ernestina and Grogan, bringing out clearly the parts they play in the plot.

12 By a close study of the relevant sections, write an account of the main aspects of Lyme Regis which you find attractive.

13 What do you learn of either (a) Victorian social conditions or (b) Victorian religion or (c) scientific discovery in the period from this novel?

14 Write about the atmosphere that John Fowles succeeds in creating in any two episodes in the novel.

15 Write about any aspect(s) of the novel not covered by any of the questions above and which you find particularly stimulating.

Further reading

Other fiction by John Fowles:
The Collector (1963)
The Aristos (1964)
The Magus (1966)
The Ebony Tower (1974)
Daniel Martin (1977)
Mantissa (1982)

The Screenplay of 'The French Lieutenant's Woman' by Harold Pinter

You might compare the novel with other modern novels, particularly those by William Golding, Iris Murdoch, Margaret Dabble, or any writer of distinction who has written in the last fifteen years.